CW01509366

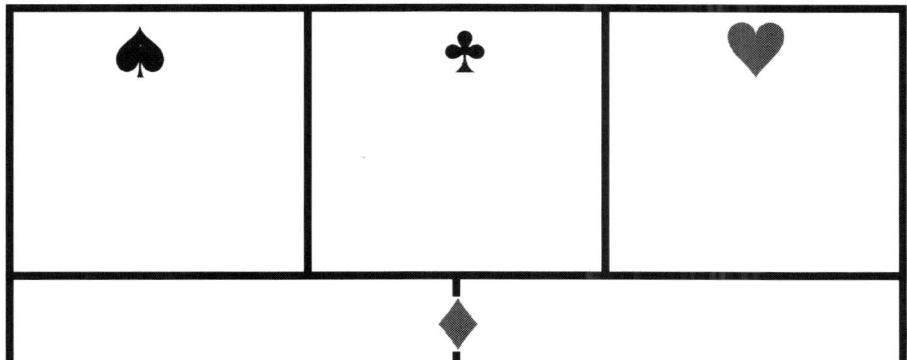

Business Model Canvas:
A Good Tool With Bad Instructions?

Rod King, PhD

(#SiliconValleyRebel)

DEDICATION

This book is dedicated to Nina and Ecy for their help and support throughout this arduous journey.

In Order to Rapidly Solve Humanity's Greatest Pains,
We Need a Shared Visual Language, Leaner Notation System, and
Simple Learning Cycle for
Rapidly Formulating and Answering Everywhere
the Pain Solving Question.

Master the O.T.H.E.R. Cycle of Genius Innovators & Polymaths (GIPs) as well as Exponential Thinking Entrepreneurs (ETE)

5 Habits of the O.T.H.E.R. Cycle

O: *Observe* what no one else is *observing*

T: *Think* what no one else is *thinking*

H: *Hypothesize* about what no one else is *hypothesizing* about

E: *Experiment* with what no one else is *experimenting* with

R: *Reflect* on what no one else is *reflecting* on

CONTENTS

Prologue: The 12 "Handicaps" of the Business Model Canvas   viii

Six Pain Solving Actors   2

1   Close Encounter with the Business Model Canvas   4

2   Evolution of the Business Model Canvas   8

3   Structure, Logic, and Applications of the Business Model Canvas   15

4   "Business Model Canvas: A Good Tool With Bad Instructions?"   20

5   Q & A Platform for Using the Business Model Canvas and its Derivatives: The Community Happiness Canvas   30

6   The Leanest Business Model Canvas: "One Page Business Plan" vs. "One Line Business Plan"   40

7   What is the Ideal Business Modeling: Business Model Tool for Answering a Pain Solving Question?   51

8   Fractal Diamond Modeling (FDM) Language: A Shorthand for Multilevel Prototyping of Pipe & Platform Projects   69

9   Predictable Disruption of the Business Model Canvas and Derivatives: The Power of Zero Time, Zero Space (ZTZS) Platforms   87

10   Why Every Value Creator Needs to Instantly Understand and Use the Visual Language of Open & Multilevel Pain Solving (OMPS)   99

11   Conclusion and Recommendation   116

Epilogue: Business Model POKER Scorecard for Open   127
Business Model Project Management (BMPM)

Bibliography   131

Appendices   133

Due to Lack of Awareness of

The "12 Handicaps" of the Business Model Canvas

As Well As

The Business Model Strip,

99% of *Business Model Canvasers* Poorly Use

The Business Model Canvas.

The Real Power of the Business Model Canvas

Lies In Its Use As

A Multilevel System Map.

PROLOGUE: THE 12 "HANDICAPS" OF THE BUSINESS MODEL CANVAS

It's been about eight years since the Business Model Canvas was first released in the book, "Business Model Generation" by Alexander Osterwalder and Yves Pigneur in collaboration with 470 practitioners from 45 countries. I was one of the collaborators.

The tool of the Business Model Canvas is now used worldwide by innovative startups as well as established companies and non-profit organizations. Yet, in these past eight years, no book has been written that critically examines the "pros" and "cons" of the Business Model Canvas. For over fifty years, the traditional voluminous business plan went unchallenged as the "standard document" for creating startups. After a perennial startup failure rate of over 70%, it has now been discovered that the traditional business plan is unsuitable for innovative startups because of its focus on "waterfall" or "tame" pain solving, planning, and execution. For innovative startups, customer pains have yet to be discovered and validated let alone be eliminated using a rigid plan or business model. It's like a doctor using a given drug to treat a patient's pain without first validating the patient's pain. In contrast, established businesses have proven or validated customer pains so that they can develop a relatively rigid plan ("prescription") for systematically growing or scaling their business model based on historical data and information. *Can such an oversight happen with the tool of the Business Model Canvas?*

Indeed, the Business Model Canvas is a good tool and it has many endorsements from highly respected people in startup communities, corporations, and academia. In a blog posting on October 25, 2010 – "Entrepreneurship as a Science – The Business Model/Customer Development Stack" - Steve Blank wrote:

"Alexander Osterwalder and Yves Pigneur defined a business model as how an organization creates, delivers, and captures value. More importantly they showed how *any company's business model could be defined in 9 boxes*. It's an amazing and powerful tool. It instantly creates a shared visual language while defining a business. Their book "Business Model Generation" is the definitive text on the subject."

But, how valid is Steve Blank's statement regarding the Business Model Canvas and its accompanying literature especially six and half years since he made that declaration? Is Steve Blank's statement valid in today's environment which is more volatile, uncertain, complex, and ambiguous and increasingly being dominated by platform (multisided/exponential market) business models rather than pipe (single market) models? Does the Business Model Canvas as well as the Business Model Generation book adequately map platforms and non-profit organizations? How well does the Business Model Canvas perform in organizations with open and "agile (fast and adaptive)" Goal Achievement Management & Experiments (GAME) systems?

In my view, the Business Model Canvas was conceived using a **paradigm of "Newtonian Space."** The monolithic "tile" layout of the Business Model Canvas is optimized for illustrating business models with single-sided markets ("pipes"). The Business Model Canvas is often presented as a visual checklist or Business Model Graphic Organizer (BMGO) that can be used to visually document, organize, and manage ideas relating to a business model (project) at a given point in time. With the focus on 9 building blocks, uses of the Business Model Canvas tend to be mechanical like in a bulleted list of elements; a large majority of users of the Business Model Canvas focuses on its parts (9 building blocks) rather than coherent or logical relationships between parts. Also, many users do not pay attention to the functioning of the whole living (sense-and-respond) system of a business model within its ecosystem and global environment. *The result is sub-optimal use of the Business Model Canvas.*

This book introduces what I call a **"Darwinstein" paradigm** for multilevel system mapping, business modeling, innovation, and performance management. With its *focus on the sense-and-respond (living system) feedback loop and continuum of SpaceTime*, the Darwinstein Paradigm introduces the dynamic concept of SpaceTime as a universal frame for organizing all ideas in systems and organizations. The Darwinstein Paradigm is manifested in a multilevel system mapping tool that is called the **"Business Model Strip."** Many shortcomings of the Business Model Canvas are revealed while doing a one-to-one comparison with the tool of the Business Model Strip, which initially maps the minimum viable elements of a system.

A table is presented below which shows some "handicaps" of the Business Model Canvas. These handicaps are presented with a view to improving performance of the Business Model Canvas especially as a tool for **Universal Pain Discovery & Solving (UPDS).**

12 "Handicaps" of the Business Model Canvas

ITEM	BUSINESS MODEL CANVAS (9-Block Business Model)	BUSINESS MODEL STRIP (One Line Business Model)
1	Static Tool: *9 Business Modeling Topics Superimposed on 9 Building Blocks/Boxes* — *Canvas requires time to sketch/set up and use*	Dynamic Tool with Feedback Loop: *4 "Sense-and Respond" Topics on 1 "Spine"* -> *Instantly Sketch & Use (Represents a Minimum Viable Business Model or Living System)*
2	Business Model Ontology/ Visual Checklist/Scorecard	Process (Sense-and-Respond & Pain Solving Cycle) Dashboard
3	Focus on Business Model Documentation	Focus on Business Model Pain Discovery & Elimination
4	Single Stakeholder (Customer) Optimization/Stories: Pipe	Multiple Stakeholder (Platform) Fitness/Stories
5	Not easy to cascade throughout an organizational hierarchy: focus is on unit of *enterprise or cost center*	Easily and rapidly cascaded throughout an organizational hierarchy: focus is on unit of *line of business, product, or service*
6	Monolithic Graphic (Canvas), Tessellation, or "Jigsaw"	Multilevel/Modular Layout; Non-/Linear Graphics
7	Rigid Business Modeling Paradigm: *Canvas* Metaphor	Flexible (Platform) Business Modeling Paradigm: *Cards*
8	Profit-focused Impacts	Shared Value (Profit- and Non-Profit) Impacts & User Exp.
9	Enterprise-facing (Supply Chain) Logic & Visual Layout	Customer & Enterprise-facing (Supply Chain) Logic
10	Limited Visual Language for Designing Platforms: *Each Line of Business Model (Pipe) is Indirect between Customer & Proposition*	Multi-pipe Visual Language & Notation System: *Goal Achievement Management & Experiment; Multilevel Pain Solving*
11	Visually Integrated with Few Business Tools	Visually Integrated with ALL Business Tools
12	Indirectly Linked to the Lean Startup Method	Directly & Fully Integrated with Lean Startup Method

"Achievement of Every Exponential Vision, Dream, or Goal on the Planet Reflects Application of the Pain-Plan-Do-Review (PPDR) or POKER Cycle."

ACKNOWLEDGMENTS

The author wishes to thank all family, friends, and acquaintances who directly and indirectly contributed to the development of ideas in this book.

As the African proverb goes, it takes a village to raise a child.

Well, nowadays, it takes a great social network to produce a successful book.
Your support is therefore invaluable

A "Living" Organizational Structure is
a Business Model is
a Project is
a Multilevel System is
a P.O.K.E.R. Cycle is
a "Sense-and-Respond" Object is
a Tool is …
For Iteratively Answering
Global Pain Solving Questions

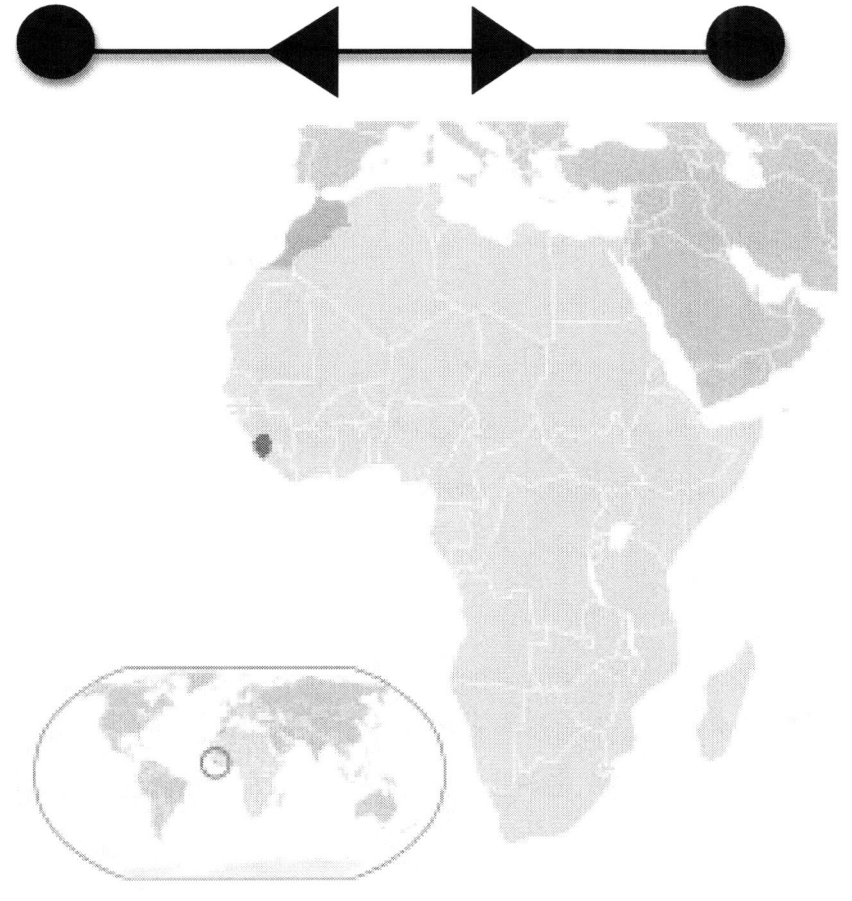

SIX PAIN SOLVING ACTORS

(Rod King's Adaptation Of Rudyard Kipling's Poem, "Six Honest Serving Men")

I KEEP a **family of six pain solving actors.**

They teach me all I know about *Open & Multilevel Pain Solving.*

They teach me how to answer **Global Pain Solving Questions**.

The parents are Timer and Spacer.

The children are Questioner and Planner and Doer and

Reviewer.

They teach me to continuously *use in Space and Time*

the Sense-and-Respond Feedback Loop or

Pain Solving Cycle: Pain-Plan-Do-Review (PPDR).

I send the family of six pain solving actors over land, sea and air,

I send them east and west; I send them north and south.

I send them everywhere; I send them all over our *fractal universe*.

But after they have scientifically and rigorously worked for me,

I give them all a rest while I sleep so that they can incubate ideas.

I let the family help me play the **Open P.O.K.E.R. Game**,

For environment is volatile, uncertain, complex, and ambiguous.

The six actors help me in improvement and innovation projects,

For the family of pain solving actors is flexible and ambidextrous.

But different folk have different views;

I know an entrepreneur in a Startup —

He apparently keeps ten million pain solving actors,

They are straight, chaotic, unscientific, and get no rest at all!

He sends 'em abroad to do Waterfall Business Planning,

No wonder all his projects are costly, long, and wasteful ... er, fail!

ALL LIFE IS PAIN SOLVING (ALIPS)

AT ITS CORE,
THIS IS A VISUAL BOOK ABOUT
**RAPIDLY FORMULATING AND ANSWERING
EVERY PAIN SOLVING QUESTION (PSQ)
IN EVERY CORNER OF OUR PLANET**

1 CLOSE ENCOUNTER WITH THE BUSINESS MODEL CANVAS

My first encounter with the visual tool of the Business Model Canvas was an accident; it was unplanned. Sometimes, fate leads us to paths that we could never have predicted especially in today's era of the Internet.

March 2009. I had been doing an Internet search for *business modeling tools* for **Universal Pain Discovery & Solving (UPDS)** when a weblink relating to "businessmodelhub.com" appeared. I clicked on it and discovered a proposal to join a community of practitioners who were interested in co-creating a book on business modeling. The community was created by the lead author, Alexander Osterwalder. At that time, there were about 150 members in that community of practice. When the book was subsequently published, there were 470 co-creators from 45 countries.

The Business Model Hub presented a unique value proposition: pre-order the book and participate in creating it. I immediately pre-ordered the book and joined the community on the Business Model Hub. I was hooked on the offer of co-creation because I was working on some very interesting ideas on business modeling as well as *universal pain (problem) solving*. My unit of research was not a "business model" per se but an "ecosystem."

When I joined the Business Model Hub, I had already developed an acronym that summarized the 9 building blocks that describe any business ecosystem. The acronym is "SEMPORCES:" **S**uppliers; **E**mployees; **M**achinery; **P**rocesses; **O**utput; **R**etailers; **C**ustomers; **E**nvironment; **S**hared Value. I had developed SEMPORCES using the logic that *every system can basically be described in terms of input, processing, and output*. For an "extended (business) system," the output is delivered through retailers to customers in an environment while creating shared value. Thus, SEMPORCES describes an extended supply chain. Alternatively, SEMPORCES could be visually presented using a multilevel "Fractal Grid" which is like an infinitely zoomable "Tic-Tac-Toe" map or 3x3 grid (tessellation) or 9 "fractal" building blocks or cards for answering any Pain Solving Question (PSQ).

SEMPORCES Fractal Grid Illustrating "Spiral" Logic of its Elements

S: Suppliers/Input	E: Employees	M: Machinery (Infra')
E: Environment	S: SHARED VALUE	P: Processes
C: Customers	R: Retailers (Distributors)	O: Outputs

After I joined the Business Model Hub, I soon realized that Alexander Osterwalder, based on his PhD dissertation, had developed an "ontology" or classification system that uses 9 building blocks to describe any business model. The 9 building blocks, which constitute what is now known as a Business Model Canvas, are described as follows: *Customer Segments; Customer Relationships; Channels; Key Partners; Value Proposition; Key Activities; Key Resources; Cost Structure; Revenue Streams*. To confirm the universality of the SEMPORCES model for pain (problem) solving and business modeling, I mapped the 9 building blocks of the Business Model Canvas on to it.

Item No.	**SEMPORCES Fractal Chain** *(Operational/Flow Focus of Topics)*	**Business Model Canvas** *(Strategic Focus of Topics)*
1	**S:** Suppliers/Inputs	Key Partners
2	**E:** Employees	Key Resources
3	**M:** Machinery (Infrastructure)	
4	**P:** Processes	Key Activities
5	**O:** Output (Product/Service)	Value Proposition
6	**R:** Retailers (Distributors)	Channels Customer Relationships
7	**C:** Customers	Customer Segments
8	**E:** Environment	
9	**S:** Shared Value	Cost Structure Revenue Streams

I observed four main differences between the SEMPORCES Chain and the Business Model Canvas. First, the building blocks of the SEMPORCES acronym are linear and reflect resource flow in a supply chain system from supplier to customer followed by the system's impact or shared value. Second, the SEMPORCES model takes a holistic approach and includes the environment as a building block while the Business Model Canvas ignores it. (In the methodology for the Business Model Canvas, the "Business Model Environment" is treated separately using another one-page model.)

The third difference was that topics of the SEMPORCES model had an operational focus while topics of the Business Model Canvas had a strategic focus. In other words, topics of the Business Model Canvas tend to be abstract. The fourth difference was in the visual display of topics. While topics of the SEMPORCES model are presented both linearly and non-linearly (as a zoomable Tic-Tac-Toe Map), the Business Model Canvas was always presented non-linearly using a network diagram. Later, the Canvas's network was replaced by a tessellation of 9 blocks which is now its standard format. The linear format of SEMPORCES facilitates comparison of business models as well as process analysis and performance management.

As mentioned earlier, the SEMPORCES model directly relates to the organization of elements in a supply chain which are usually presented using a SIPOC diagram. SIPOC is an acronym for Supplier; Input; Process; Output; Customer. Below is presented a "New SIPOC Template" which includes an additional element of "Channel." Consequently, the new template has the acronym, SIPOCC.

To better understand the workflow in a SEMPORCES model, elements of SEMPORCES are categorized using the SIPOCC diagram below. With a diagram showing the SIPOCC Chain as well as SEMPORCES Chain, one could better align tools of business process improvement with tools of business model improvement and innovation.

New SIPOC Template and Supply Chain Logic of "SEMPORCES"

<u>**SIPOCC Chain**</u>

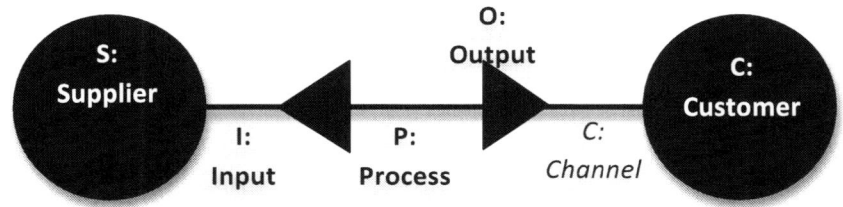

<u>**SEMPORCES Chain**</u>

Suppliers/Input   Output   Customer

Employees   Process   Retailers

Machinery

(Infra')

SHARED VALUE   ENVIRONMENT

The above diagram and approach are paradigm-shifting for many users of the modeling tools such as the Business Model Canvas do not see a direct connection between business modeling and tools such as the Business Model Canvas and tools for business process improvement and innovation such as the SIPOC diagram and Fishbone ("Ishikawa") diagram. All are tools that model a system at different levels.

Although the classic Business Model Canvas is always illustrated using an irregular grid, jigsaw, or tessellation, it can also be presented using a "tic-tac-toe" board or 3x3 (fractal) grid. The "tic-tac-toe," tessellated, or jigsaw-layout of the Business Model Canvas may appear 'monolithic.' However, as a fractal grid, each card can be regarded as independent and as a tic-tac-toe. In other words, the whole Business Model Canvas-Fractal Grid as well as each of the 9 cards has a 3x3 (tic-tac-toe) structure. This fractal grid structure supports modular, distributed, or open pain (problem) solving which requires both separate and collaborative pain (problem) discovery and solving. Also, it is easy to visualize the Business Model Canvas-Fractal Grid as a "card" of the Business Model Ecosystem which is in turn a "card" of the Global Environment.

Business Model Canvas-Fractal Grid: 9 Categories ("Cards") of Business Modeling Topics *("Business Model Environment" is additional topic)*

KP: Key Partners	**KR1:** Key Resources1	**KR2:** Key Resources2
BME: Business Model Environment	**C$:** Cost Structure **R$:** Revenue Streams	**KA:** Key Activities
CS: Customer Segments	**CH:** Channels **CR:** Customer Relationships	**VP:** Value Proposition

The different visualizations of the SEMPORCES model and Business Model Canvas indicate that while visual configurations are different, the underlying system logic of a business model is unchanged. Nevertheless, each visualization has a trade-off that must be considered when choosing a visual format for displaying or presenting a business model.

2 EVOLUTION OF THE BUSINESS MODEL CANVAS

The origin of the Business Model Canvas lies in the PhD dissertation that Alexander Osterwalder published in 2004 at the University of Lausanne in Switzerland. The title of his dissertation of 172 pages is: *"The Business Model Ontology: A Proposition in a Design Science Approach."* He later released a PDF version on the Internet. Osterwalder dedicates his thesis to "All those people out there fighting poverty in the world."

In his dissertation, Osterwalder came up with a synthesis of 9 topics, which are visually arranged using a network (concept) diagram, to describe how any business model works. The network diagram, then known as a **"Business Model Template"** inherently had two levels. The lower level of the Business Model Template featured 9 building blocks: *Target Customer; Customer Relationship; Distribution Channel; Partner Network; Value Proposition; Core Capabilities; Value Configuration; Cost Structure; Revenue Streams.* At the higher or macro-level, the 9 building blocks are visually organized into four categories: *Infrastructure; Offer; Customer; Finance.* These macro-categories, which correspond to the four question-tags of *How; What; Who; Why*, are reminiscent of the four perspectives of the Balanced Scorecard: *Learning & Growth, Internal Processes, Customer, and Financial Perspectives.*

Business Model Template (Osterwalder: 2004)

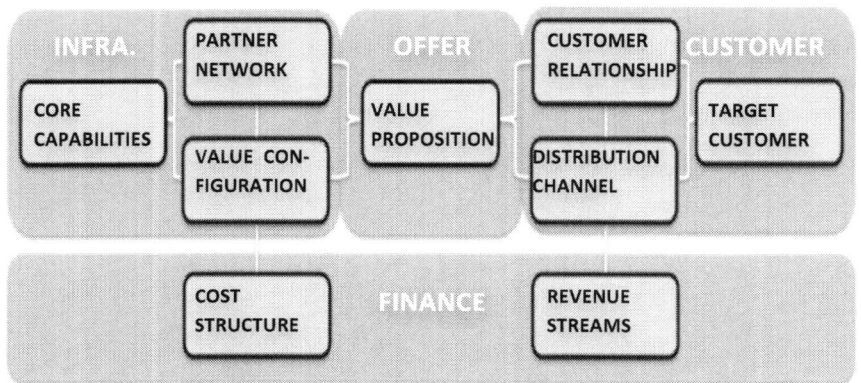

It is important to note that the above Business Model Template presents a *dual macro-structure*: the top part of the template describes an "extended business system" or "supply chain" while the lower part describes the (financial) impact of the system. This is why the model is so versatile.

The content of the co-created **"Business Model Generation"** book reflects four important changes to the Business Model Template. First, the name of the tool is changed to "Business Model Canvas." Second, the graphic network diagram is replaced by a tessellation or "jigsaw" of 9 blocks; linkages between blocks are omitted in the Business Model Canvas. Third, five of the original descriptions are modified: from *"Target Customer"* to *"Customer Segment"*; from *"Distribution Channel"* to *"Channel"*; from *"Partner Network"* to *"Key Partners"*; from *"Core Capabilities"* to *"Key Activities"*; from *"Value Configuration"* to *"Key Resources."*. Fourth, the initial topic in the Business Template is "Core Capabilities" while the Business Model Canvas starts with the topic of "Key Partners." Consequently, the Business Model Canvas reflect a more coherent supply chain logic than the Business Model Template.

Business Model Canvas (Osterwalder: 2009)

Key Partners (KP)	Key Activities (KA)	Value Proposition (VP)	Customer Relation-ships (CR)	Customer Segments (CS)
	Key Resources (KR)		Channels (CH)	
Cost Structure (C$)			Revenue Streams (R$)	

In his PhD dissertation, Osterwalder defines a business model as follows:

"A business model is a conceptual tool that contains a set of elements and their relationships and allows expressing a company's logic of earning money."
He adds,
"It is a description of the value a company offers to one or several segments of customers and the architecture of the firm and its network of partners for creating, marketing and delivering this value and relationship capital, in order to generate profitable and sustainable revenue streams."

A more succinct description of a business model is presented in the Business Model Generation Book. In that book, Osterwalder et al state:
"A business model describes the rationale of how an organization creates, delivers, and captures value."

It is important to note that while the dissertation's definition of a business model focuses on finance and in particular "earning money," the definition of a business model in the Business Model Generation book focuses on value. This distinction is important because the concept of a business model applies to for-profit organizations as well as not-for-profit organizations. Nevertheless, the traditional focus of the Business Model Canvas deals with documenting and understanding businesses with a profit motive and strategy. The Business Model Generation book does not present any example on the business model of a not-for-profit organization.

Since initial publication of the Business Model Generation book in 2009, there has been myriad derivatives or customizations of the Business Model Canvas with regard to topics as well as visual layout of the Canvas. The most popular derivative is the **Lean Canvas** by Ash Maurya. Recognizing that the Business Model Canvas tacitly assumes that an organization has a proven or validated business model, Maurya focused on designing a Canvas that highlights business model search or discovery for startups rather than business model understanding or improvement. Startups use an iterative process of customer pain finding as well as pain solving to discover profitable business models. So, Maurya replaced four topics on the Business Model Canvas with the following: *Problem; Solution; Key Metrics; Unfair Advantage*. He modified "Value Proposition" to *"Unique Value Proposition."*

It must be noted that neither the Business Model Canvas nor the Lean Canvas uses a Question-and-Answer (Q & A) approach that poses a strategy or macro-question that the Canvas should answer. Rather, hints, micro-questions, or notes are used to provide guidelines on the content that should be placed in each of the 9 building blocks. *Profit is the desired impact.*

Lean Canvas (Ash Maurya: 2009)

Problem	Solution	*Unique* Value Proposition	Unfair Advantage	Customer Segments
	Key Metrics		Channels	
Cost Structure			Revenue Streams	

In order to address the needs of (lean) startups in their process of business model search or discovery, Osterwalder et al developed a "plug in" called the "Value Proposition Canvas." Although the Value Proposition Canvas can be used as a stand alone tool for finding Problem-Solution Fitness as well as Product-Market Fitness, it directly relates to two blocks of the Business Model Canvas: *Value Proposition* and *Customer Segments*. The Value Proposition Canvas can therefore be considered as an integral ("zoomed in") part of the Business Model Canvas. Note that on the Value Proposition Canvas, the two blocks are respectively named *"Value Map"* and *"Customer Profile."* The Value Map includes **trade-off (features) associated with functionality** of Products & Services while the Customer Profile includes **trade-off of jobs to get done** of customer segment(s).

Value Proposition Canvas (Osterwalder et al: 2014)

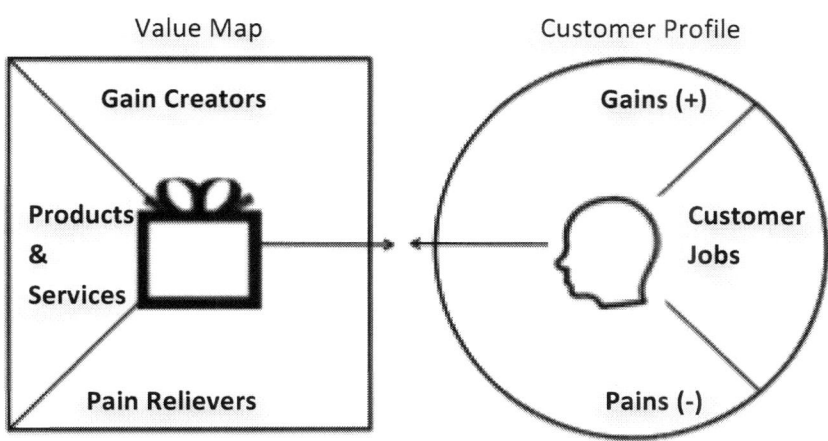

With regard to non-for-profit organizations, Alexander Osterwalder and Steve Blank customized the Business Model Canvas and created a **"Mission Model Canvas"** in 2016. While maintaining the system logic of the Business Model Canvas, the Mission Model Canvas focuses on using terms that "make sense" to Mission-driven Organizations. For instance, "Customer Segment" is replaced by *"Beneficiaries."* Unlike in the Business Model Canvas, the Mission Model Canvas has the overarching topic of *"Mission (or "problem") definition."* The Mission Model Canvas is therefore couched in the paradigm of Pain Discovery and Solving. Most importantly, the Mission Canvas focuses on *Cost Effectiveness* rather than *Financial Profit.* Consequently, topics of "Cost Effectiveness" of the Mission Model Canvas are *Mission Budget (Cost)* and *Mission Achievement (Fulfillment/Impact) Factors or Criteria.* In general, Impact can be described in terms of *"Cost"* and *"Benefit."*

Mission Model Canvas (Osterwalder & Blank: 2016)

Mission (or "Problem") Description: ....

Key Partners	Key Activities	Value Proposition	Buy-in & Support	Beneficiaries
	Key Resources		Deployment	
Mission Budget (or Cost)		Mission Achievement (or "Fulfillment or "Impact) Factors (or Criteria)		

Three years after publishing the "Business Model Generation" book, Ostwerwalder et al published a business model related book for personal career development. The book, which has the title of **"Business Model You,"** is positioned as *"A one-page tool to reinvent yourself and your career."* In that book, the Business Model Canvas is reframed as a "Personal Business Model Canvas." The main differences relate to the topics of Finance. In the Personal Business Model Canvas, the topic of *"Cost"* replaces "Cost Structure" while *"Revenue and Benefits"* replace "Revenue Structure." Nevertheless, it is in the note or annotation of each block that the Personal Business Model Canvas differs significantly from annotations in the Business Model Canvas. The annotations in the former are more personal.

Personal Business Model Canvas (Osterwalder et al: 2012)

Key Partners (KP) *Who helps you*	Key Activities (KA) *What you do*	Value Proposition (VP) *How you help*	Customer Relation-ships (CR) *How you interact*	Customer Segments (CS) *Who you help*
	Key Resources (KR) *Who you are and what you have*		Channels (CH) *How they know you and how you deliver*	
Cost Structure (C$) *What you give*			Revenue Streams (R$) *What you get*	

The tool of the Business Model Canvas continues to evolve both in terms of its original topics and visual layout. There seems to be a bespoke or customized canvas for different groups of professionals or project. This mass customization is inevitable since different domains use different registers of words for pain discovery and solving. For instance, in the not-for-profit sector, people speak in terms of *beneficiaries* rather than *customers* although each is a *value recipient*.. Also, for-profit organizations traditionally evaluate impacts in financial terms and in particular, *cost* and *revenue*. In contrast, not-for profit organizations evaluate impacts in terms of *cost* and *effectiveness (social benefit)*.

Some modifications of the original Business Model Canvas have more than 9 topics or building blocks; further topics/building blocks have been added. In March 2016, students of the Master's program, "MFA in Products of Design" at New York City's School of Visual Arts (SVA), did a project on reimagining the Business Model Canvas; their work can be seen at: http://productsofdesign.sva.edu/blog/2016/2/29/reimagining-the-business-model-canvas

Some derivative canvases adhere to the topics and visual system logic of the Business Model Canvas while others do not. My conclusion is that there is and will be no standard visual format for expressing the logic of a business model. At its core, a business model is an *extended system or a customer-focused tool for viably achieving a project's mission, vision, goal, objective, or strategy*. In short, business modeling is in the "Business Of Goal Achievement (BOGA)." I perceive a Business Model Canvas as a visual and collaborative tool for facilitating **Universal Pain Discovery & Solving (UPDS)**.

3 STRUCTURE, LOGIC, AND APPLICATIONS OF THE BUSINESS MODEL CANVAS

This chapter focuses on answering two categories of questions:

"Is there only one visual level of 9 building blocks for the Business Model Canvas?

"Why is the Business Model Canvas applicable to so many different types of projects in for-profit sector as well as non-profit sector?"

If there is one thing that is fairly constant in Osterwalder's development of the Business Model Canvas, it's the number of topics for comprehensively describing any business model. Since publishing his "Business Model Template," Osterwalder has stuck to the magic number of "9" topics. However, this is a granular description of the topics for describing a business model. At a higher level of abstraction, Osterwalder uses four categories to organize the 9 topics of the Business Model Canvas:

- **INFRASTRUCTURE:** *Key Activities; Key Resources; Key Partners*
- **OFFER:** *Value Proposition*
- **CUSTOMER:** *Customer Segments; Channel; Customer Relationships*
- **FINANCE:** *Cost Structure; Revenue Streams*

"Meso-Canvas Template" is my description of the higher level template that is directly derived from the Business Model Canvas. As is seen below, the Meso-Canvas is a tessellation or "jigsaw board" with 5 meso-blocks. This visual template can be used as a pre-formatted visual checklist for purposes other than in business modeling. The tessellated format facilitates collaborative work especially using sticky (Post-It) notes.

Meso-Canvas Template (5 Meso-blocks)

The four categories of topics or "disciplines" of the Business Model Canvas are now presented using the Meso-Canvas Template.

Meso-Canvas with 4 "Disciplines" of Business Model Topics

INFRASTRUCTURE	OFFER	CUSTOMER
FINANCE		

In the Meso-Canvas below, the 9 business modeling topics are organized using the four main *disciplines*; each discipline directly relates to a question-tag. Inclusion of the question-tags facilitates the understanding that a Business Model Canvas describes a scene, snapshot, or system of a project at a given point in time. It is this *ubiquitous story structure or system narrative* that gives the Business Model Canvas its power of versatility.

Had the main topic of "Finance" been replaced with **"Viability,"** the power of the Business Model Canvas would have been awesome. Using "Viability" enables the same canvas to be used in determining or managing any type of project viability or impact (pain (-); delight (+)); for instance, *financial viability; social viability; environmental viability.* There would have been fewer types of canvases, many of which do not display the **visual system logic** of the original Business Model Template or Business Model Canvas.

Meso-Canvas with 4 "Disciplines" and 9 Business Modeling Topics

INFRASTRUCTURE *(HOW)*	OFFER *(WHAT)*	CUSTOMER *(WHO)*
○ *Key Resources* ○ *Key Activities* ○ *Key Partners*	○ *Value Proposition*	○ *Customer Segments* ○ *Channels* ○ *Customer Relationships*
FINANCE		
○ *Cost Structure*	*(WHY)* ○ *Revenue Streams*	

Based on my research on universal system models, I developed the visual template of a **Business Model Loop (Strip)** which illustrates **how any system with a basic feedback loop works to resolve pain**. In other words, a Business Model Loop illustrates a basic cybernetic system. *A sustainable business model is a dynamic extended system with net positive feedback loop.*

The four nodes of a Business Model Strip are as follows: **Value Creator; Output; Value Recipient; Feedback (Impact: -/+)**. The link between any two nodes is described as a **channel**. To illustrate why the visual structure of the Business Model Canvas works, I replace the four main categories of the Business Model Canvas with descriptions of the four nodes of a Business Model Strip. Again, *we see why the Canvas is so versatile.*

Meso-Canvas with Descriptions of 4 "Cybernetic" Perspectives and 9 Business Modeling Topics For Answering a Pain Solving Question

VALUE CREATOR (HOW)	OUTPUT (WHAT)	VALUE RECEIVER (WHO)
o *Key Resources* o *Key Activities* o *Key Partners*	o *Value Proposition*	o *Customer Segments* o *Channels* o *Customer Relationships*
FEEDBACK, IMPACT (-/+), PERFORMANCE METRICS, or VIABILITY o *Cost Structure* (WHY) o *Revenue Streams*		

At the highest level of abstraction, we can say that a Business Model Loop describes a *sense-and-respond relationship* between an Extended System and Feedback (Impact: -/+; Viability). We can use a three macro-block canvas and present it at two levels: upper stage (superstructure) and lower stage (foundation). This is the *dual structure of all living systems or organizations.*

Macro-Canvas Template Illustrating *Macro "Sense-and-Response" Loop*

EXTENDED SYSTEM (VALUE CREATOR; OUTPUT; VALUE RECEIVER)
FEEDBACK, IMPACT (-/+), PERFORMANCE METRICS, or VIABILITY

When we compare the visual structure of the Meso- and Macro-Canvas, we see that it is for the description of the superstructure or extended system that the number of blocks usually varies. The Macro-Canvas uses one "upper" block while the Meso-Canvas uses three "upper" blocks as information holders for describing an extended system. The classic format of the Business Model Canvas uses 7 "upper" blocks. Consequently, the classic Business Model Canvas uses greater granularity for describing the extended system of a business model.

A disadvantage of the Business Model Canvas's classic format of 9 tessellated blocks is that no visual hierarchy is shown: the structure of the meso-canvas is not highlighted. Absence of this meso-structure causes many users to misinterpret and misuse the classic Business Model Canvas. Nevertheless, one can easily add a visual hierarchy to the Business Model Canvas by thickening the borders of building blocks of the meso-canvas.

Template of Business Model Canvas (Shown with Visual Hierarchy)

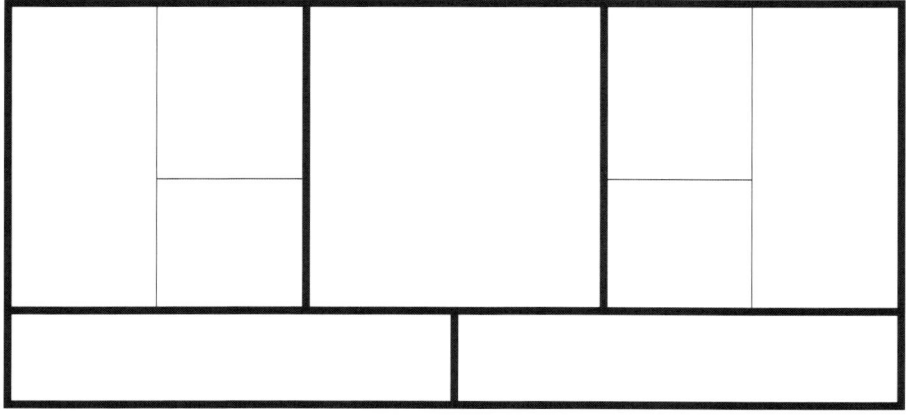

It is important to note that while the Business Model Template visually illustrates the four categories as well as 9 blocks, the classic Business Model Canvas does away will illustrating and naming the four categories. Instead, the Business Model Canvas focuses on presenting 9 topics and 9 building blocks. The *apparent association of one topic with one building block* has created the illusion of equivalence between a topic and a building block. In other words, in the world of the Business Model Canvas, a business modeling topic seems to be synonymous with a building block. This is a fallacy that restricts novel design and applications of the Canvas. Nevertheless, there are cognitive advantages especially in ease of understanding and documentation in having one business topic per building block.

Having discussed the multilevel structure of the Business Model Canvas, we can turn our attention to areas of application of the Business Model Canvas. To date, the areas of application of the Business Model Canvas as well as its derivatives are too numerous to mention. Rather, we shall organize areas of application according to two dimensions - *maturity of project* and *viability motive* - for answering any Pain Solving Question (PSQ).

Portfolio of Applications for Business Model Canvas & Ancillary Tools

VIABILITY MOTIVE PROJECT MATURITY		**For-Profit** Sector (Business Only)	**Non-Profit** Sector (Pure; Hybrid)
INNOVATION PROJECTS: Novel or Disruptive Product/ Service/ Business Model *(Disruptive Innovation; Blue Ocean Strategy)*	*"Pipe"* Business Model: 1-sided market	Business Model Canvas; Value Proposition Canvas; Personal Business Model Canvas	
	"Platform" Business Model: 2/Multi-sided market	Business Model Canvas; Value Proposition Canvas	Mission Model Canvas; Value Proposition Canvas
IMPROVEMENT PROJECTS: Existing or Proven Product/ Service/ Business Model *(Strategic/Business Planning; Competitive Strategy; Red Ocean Strategy)*	*"Pipe"* Business Model	Business Model Canvas; Value Proposition Canvas; Personal Business Model Canvas	
	"Platform" Business Model: 2/Multi-sided market	Business Model Canvas; Value Proposition Canvas	Mission Model Canvas; Value Proposition Canvas

In summary, a Business Model Canvas can be presented using a visual template, at least, at three levels: *Macro-Canvas (3 blocks); Meso-Canvas (5 blocks); Classic Business Model Canvas (9 blocks).* The versatility of the Business Model Canvas is due to its inherent *business model (extended system) or "cybernetic" feedback loop* that is reflected in the description of the 9 topics as well as inherent meso-level structure of the Business Model Canvas.

4 "BUSINESS MODEL CANVAS: A GOOD TOOL WITH BAD INSTRUCTIONS?"

In this chapter, I reproduce the original article with the same title as this chapter's (as well as this book's). On January 20, 2017, I first posted the article on LinkedIn and it generated global interest. It was people's positive and encouraging reactions as well as their enthusiastic sharing of the article that inspired me to write this book.

Here's the article …

Alexander Osterwalder's **Business Model Canvas** is widely used by entrepreneurs around the world. It is a good tool. It is a good visual checklist of the elements of a business model or an "extended enterprise." However, the B*usiness Model Canvas is not great because it does not explicitly focus on solving the pain of stakeholders in a given project.* Also, the Business Model Canvas has not enhanced *deep learning* of **"Business Model Innovation & Improvement (BMII)."** The vast majority of users of the Business Model Canvas display *surface learning* regarding BMII and in particular, continuous Business Model Pain Solving.

Surface learning of the Business Model Canvas has led to the proliferation of business model-like canvases: *there seems to be a new canvas for every goal, objective, or type of project.* The Business Model Canvas is in the **"Business Of Goal Achievement (BOGA)."** However, that idea has not yet fully dawned on many practitioners including the creators of the Business Model Canvas and its derivatives.

Currently, the Business Model Canvas is solution (value proposition)-focused rather than pain (problem) discovery, learning, and elimination-focused. The Business Model Canvas is driven by the Value Proposition, which <u>assumes that a stated Value Proposition is the desired solution, tactic, or offering for resolving the pain of the stated targeted customer</u>. The Business Model Canvas also neglects a **Customer-focused Strategy**, from which a **pain-centered Value Proposition** can be derived.

At best, the **customer Job To Get Done, Business Strategy, and Value Proposition** should focus on continuously solving a **"Big Urgent Market Pain (BUMP)."** To iterate, the Business Model Canvas is not a direct tool for comprehensive pain (problem) discovery, learning, and solving. The *Business Model Canvas also lacks inherent focus on a process for facilitating experimentation, prototyping, and execution of projects.*

The Business Model Canvas was not developed as a tool for facilitating application of the **paradigm of Pain Discovery, Learning, and Elimination**, which is reminiscent of the "scientific method for discovering and solving problems." Rather, the Business Model Canvas was originally conceived as a 'scorecard' that uses a shared visual language for documenting a business model and with a view to developing a shared understanding of an organization's business model at a given point in time. A Business Model Canvas provides a 'snapshot' of a business. Consequently, the Business Model Canvas is 'time agnostic:' it can be used for documenting past, present, and future business models. In theory, the Business Model Canvas is a visual synthesis of topics for comprehensively describing a business model and project as well as a system and its impacts. Nevertheless, flows or exchanges between building blocks are not shown on the Business Model Canvas which is presented as a **tessellation or "Treemap" of 9 blocks**.

In their book, "Business Model Generation," Alexander Osterwalder and Yves Pigneur suggest two processes for using the Business Model Canvas. The first process consists of three steps: 1) Plot the Canvas 2) Put the poster on the wall 3) Sketch out your business model. The second process, which is called the "Business Model Design Process," is more detailed and consists of five steps: 1) Mobilize 2) Understand 3) Design 4) Implement 5) Manage.

It is probably the first process that has contributed to the ad hoc and unfocused use of the Business Model Canvas. The Business Model Design Process, which is more systematic and focused, is reminiscent of IDEO's Design Thinking Process of Empathize, Define, Ideate, Prototype, and Test. The Business Model Process goes one step further with "Manage." However, the Business Model Design Process is neither lean in terms of use of resources nor explicitly focused on eliminating the pain of stakeholders especially customers. Also, the Business Model Design Process targets established companies rather than startups.

Recognizing the deficit of the Business Model Canvas with regard to pain (problem) discovery and solving, several practitioners have tried to modify or "patch" it as well as add complementary tools and processes. In his Customer Development Stack, Steve Blank adds the process of Customer Development to facilitate pain discovery. He also adds Agile

Development (Lean Startup) Method to facilitate experimentation and testing of hypotheses from a "Future (Hypothetical) Business Model Canvas." Even Osterwalder himself has developed the tool of "Value Proposition Canvas" to augment the pain (problem) discovery and solving capability of the Business Model Canvas.

Ash Maurya has modified building blocks of the Business Model Canvas to suit the mindset and language of "Lean Startup" entrepreneurs as well as directly include the paradigm of pain (problem) solving. Maurya includes building blocks such as for "Problem," "Solution," and "Key Metrics." However, Maurya's location of building blocks such as "Unfair Advantage" violate the visual system logic of the Business Model Canvas.

To date, many entrepreneurs are busy and sometimes, mindlessly completing building blocks of the Business Model Canvas without a clear pain (problem) solving process. The Build-Measure-Learn Loop of the Lean Startup Method can be used with the Business Model Canvas. However, to date the Lean Startup Method which includes the process of "Innovation Accounting" has not been seamlessly integrated with the logic and building blocks of the Business Model Canvas.

Without 'proper' instructions, entrepreneurs the world over have been ineffectively using the Business Model Canvas especially as *just a visual checklist of the elements of a business model or an extended enterprise*. The result is enormous waste of money, energy, and time while trying to rapidly discover and solve the pain of stakeholders especially customers. So, what are we to do?

This article introduces the **Pain-Plan-Do-Review (PPDR) Cycle** which can be used with or without the Business Model Canvas. Housing the PPDR Cycle is the **Community Happiness Canvas** which presents a Pain Solving Question (PSQ) that is answered by using a multilevel hierarchy of topics: from the *two parts (question-and-answer) of the* **PSQ and PPDR Cycle** *through the five "fingers" of the* **Total Design Thinking (TDT) Cycle** *to the 9 topics of* **LIST** (List of Innovate Salone Topics).

The LIST largely consists of topics from GMin's application form of applicants to the community innovation program for school-going students in Sierra Leone, Kenya, and South Africa. Dozens of innovation projects have been successfully completed using the structure and content of the LIST. Unique features of the LIST include its consideration of the topics of "Problem/Challenge/Pain" and "Other Solutions." Further, topics of the

LIST inherently reflect the iterative paradigm of Pain Discovery, Learning, and Elimination.

The presentation below shows correspondences between topics of the Business Model Canvas and Community Happiness Canvas. The Community Happiness Canvas is a visual platform that *can be used to "plug-and-play" any business tool including* Brainstorming, Golden Circle, Design Thinking, Customer Development, the Business Model Canvas, Lean Canvas, and Lean Startup Method. The Community Happiness Canvas therefore provides a universal visual language for all pain solvers: Brainstormers; Marketers; Six Sigma Practitioners; Design Thinkers; Business Modelers; Entrepreneurs; Managers; Executives.

A "Question-and-Answer Platform" for Using the Business Model Canvas & its Derivatives: The Community Happiness Canvas

Business Model Canvas: Topics/Questions *(Elements of Extended Enterprise/ System)*	**Community Happiness Canvas:** Topics *(Pain-Plan-Do-Review (PPDR) Cycle; Ecosystem)*
1. **Customer Segments** (CS)	**PAIN SOLVING QUESTION (PSQ):** *How Might We Eliminate Pain (HMWEP) of "X"?*
2. **Customer Relationships** (CR)	1. **PAIN** (Collect; *Empathize; Define*)
	1.1 **Problem/Challenge/Pain**
3. **Channels** (CH)	1.2 Customers/Stakeholders
	1.3 **Other Solutions**
4. **Key Partners** (KP)	2. **PLAN** (To Do: **Ideas**; *Ideate*)
	2.1 Proposed Solution (End)
5. **Value Proposition** (VP)	2.2 Plan of Action (Ways)
	2.3 Resources (Means)
6. **Key Activities** (KA)	3. **DO** (Doing: **Build/ Prototype; Measure;** *Test*)
7. **Key Resources** (KR)	4. **REVIEW** (Done: **Learn;** Innovation Accounting)
8. **Cost Structure** (C$)	4.1 Budget: COST (STRUCTURE)
9. **Revenue Streams** (R$)	4.2 Motivation: BENEFITS – REVENUE (STREAMS)

By using the PPDR Cycle of the Community Happiness Canvas in conjunction with the topics of the Business Model Canvas, entrepreneurs can rapidly discover and solve the pains of stakeholders especially customers. By solving widely experienced pains at a price that targeted customers can afford, entrepreneurs can rapidly build profitable business models that can scale. A simpler or more organic approach to incorporate "pain solving thinking" while using the Business Model Canvas is to initially pose a **Pain Solving Question (PSQ)** which is in the format of: *"How Might We Eliminate Pain (HMWEP) of 'X'?"* The symbol "X" represents any of the 9 building blocks as well as any element in the Business Model Environment.

Every time an experiment or testing of a business model hypothesis is completed, the entrepreneur should check whether a targeted pain has been eliminated. Thereafter, the entrepreneur must decide whether to persevere with reducing the targeted pain or to pivot to another pain for elimination. A Pain Solving Question simply provides a framework that justifies iterative pain solving while using the Business Model Canvas.

So, what do you think?

****

PS. Lack of process-focus in using the Business Model Canvas has created an *unhealthy* fixation on the tessellation of the Business Model Canvas as the 'only' way to visually present the topics of a business model. One advantage of a tessellation is *spatial efficiency*, since the blocks efficiently cover a given space. Another advantage of a tessellation is that its graphic can be used horizontally (on a table) as well as vertically (on a wall). Today, there are countless variations of the 9-block tessellation of the Business Model Canvas.

With its focus on process and in particular, the Pain-Plan-Do-Review (PPDR) Cycle, topics of the Community Happiness Canvas can be presented in **visual formats ranging from a 'chain' through a 'macro-canvas' and 'tree' to a 'network.'** The presentation below shows visual templates that can be used for topics of the Community Happiness Canvas.

<u>Note</u>
The original LinkedIn article can be found here:
https://www.linkedin.com/pulse/business-model-canvas-good-tool-bad-instructions-rod-king-ph-d-?trk=pulse_spock-articles

Typology of Visual Templates for Presenting Topics/ Elements of a SpaceTime System (Map): Business Model, Supply Chain, and Pain-Plan-Do-Review (PPDR) Cycle

1. Business Model **Chain** (List; Stack System)

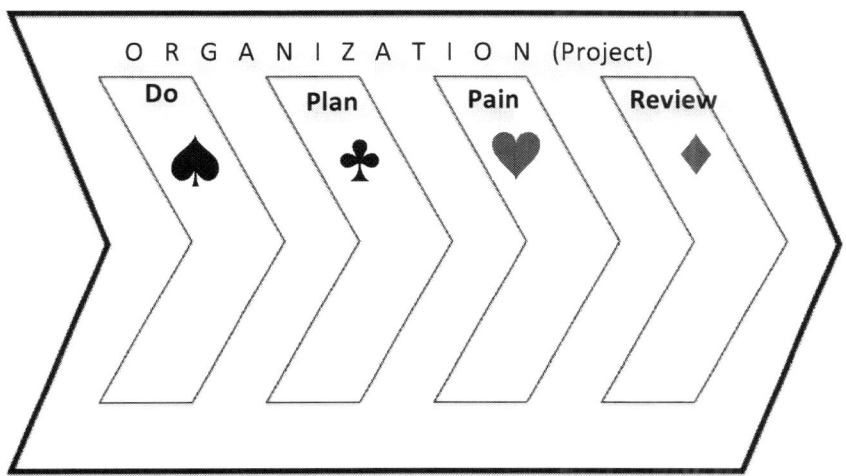

2. Business Model **Meso-Canvas** (Theater; House; Jigsaw; Chain System)

Organization (Project): ....

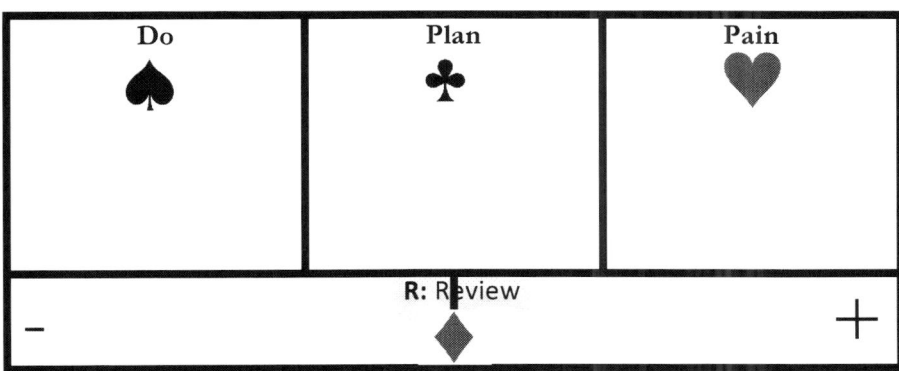

3. Business Model **Tree** (Mind Map; Hub; Fractal Brain System)

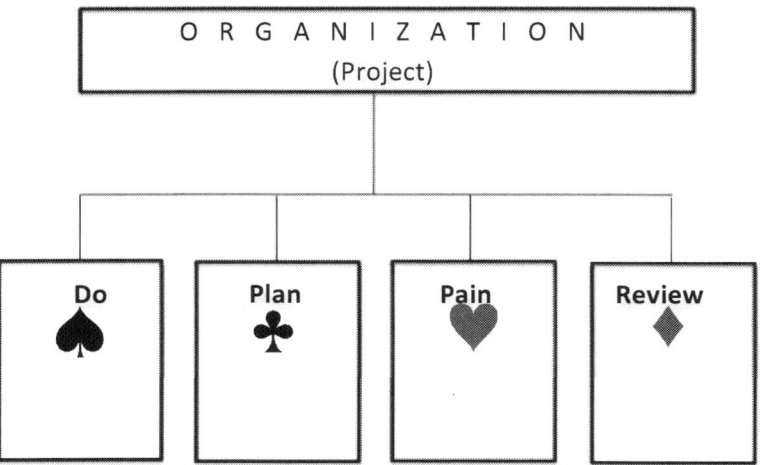

4. Business Model **Network** (Molecule; Diamond; Pyramid; Periodic Table; Neural Brain System)

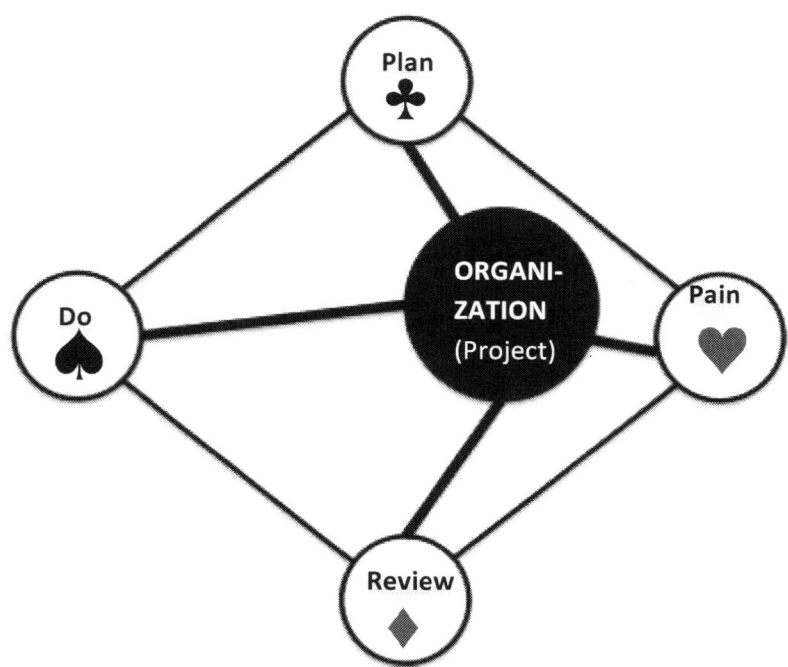

About a month after writing the foregoing article, I elaborated on the PPDR Cycle to directly focus on the Objectives & Key Results (OKR) Framework that is used for Open Pain Solving in organizations such as Google, LinkedIn, Intel, and Uber. The term "Plan" in the Pain-Plan-Do-Review (PPDR) Cycle is replaced by "Objectives" and "Results" while term "Do" is replaced by "Experiments." So, the POKER Cycle refers to *Pain-Objectives-Key Results-Experiments-Review.*

A POKER cycle can be expressed in linear and non-linear formats. Below, the POKER cycle is presented using a meso- and micro-canvas. The POKER Canvas can be used to succinctly describe a process for eliminating pain in organizations as well as scalably present the building blocks of a business model such as in the Business Model Canvas.

POKER Canvas (5 Meso-blocks)

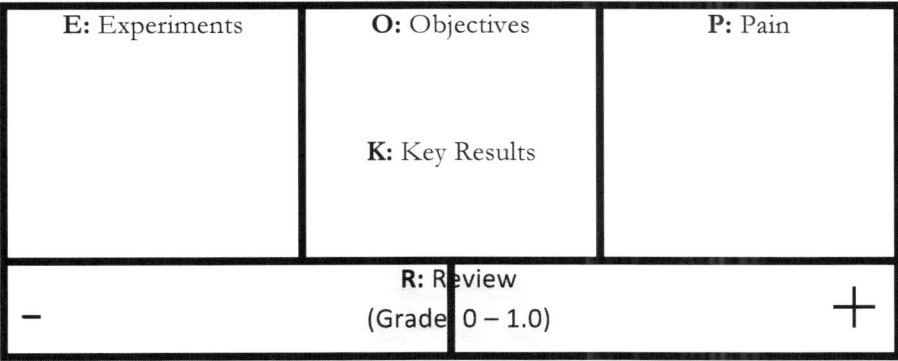

POKER Canvas (9 Micro-blocks)

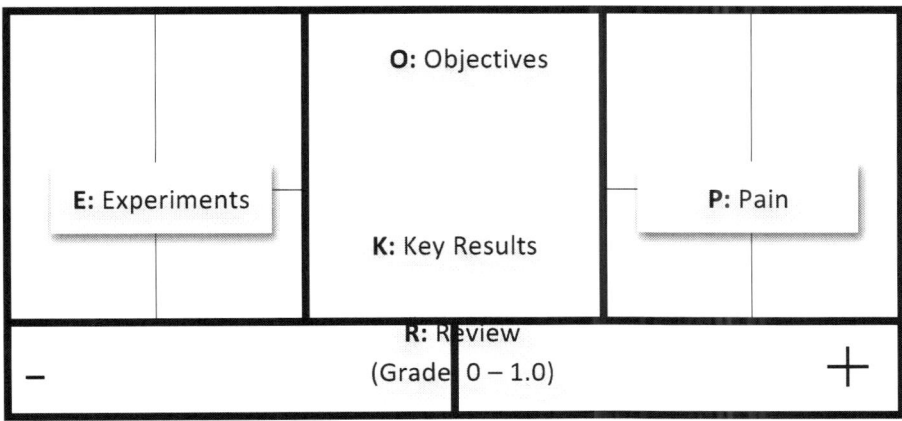

Below the POKER Canvas is presented using the symbols of playing cards.

POKER Canvas (5 Meso-blocks) *with Symbols of Playing Cards*

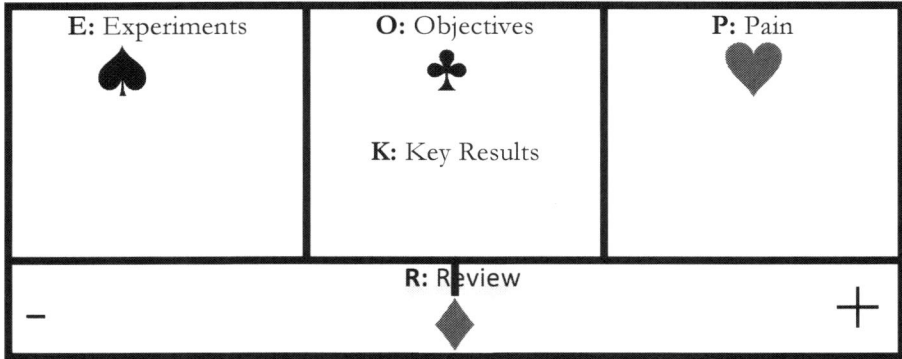

POKER Template (5 Meso-blocks) *with Only Symbols of Playing Cards*

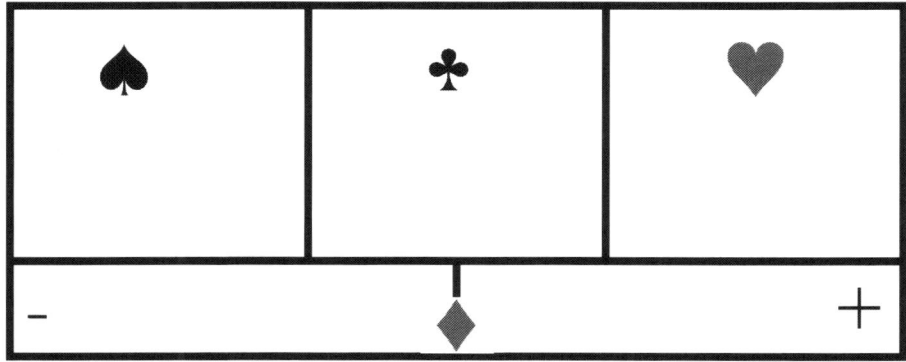

POKER <u>**Template**</u> (9 Micro-blocks) *with Only Symbols of Playing Cards*

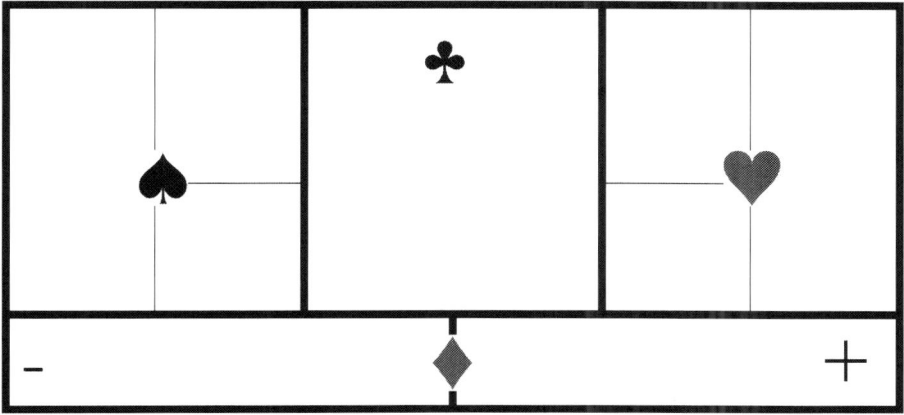

5 Q & A PLATFORM FOR USING THE BUSINESS MODEL CANVAS & ITS DERIVATIVES: THE COMMUNITY HAPPINESS CANVAS

A classic Business Model Canvas is shown below but with a highlighted visual hierarchy showing five macro-blocks: *three upper macro-blocks (value creator; output; value recipient) and two lower macro-blocks (cost viability and benefit viability)*. The visual hierarchy facilitates discussion regarding the **"cybernetic (feedback)" system logic or extended supply chain** of the Business Model Canvas as well as the **dynamic viability** of a given business model. So, given such a *dually structured* Business Model Canvas, how should one start using it?

Classic Business Model Canvas: 9 Business Modeling Topics and Building Blocks for Answering a Pain Solving Question - *"How Might We Eliminate Pain (HMWEP) of X?"* ... *X is any topic or organization*

Key Partners (KP)	Key Activities (KA)	Value Proposition (VP)	Customer Relation-ships (CR)	Customer Segments (CS)
	Key Resources (KR)		Channels (CH)	
Cost Structure (C$)			Revenue Streams (R$)	

Source: https://en.wikipedia.org/wiki/Business_Model_Canvas

With regard to using a Business Model Canvas, the Business Model Generation book contains two processes: a three-step generic process and five-step design process. The three-step process can be used to answer three time-based questions:

➤ PAST: How <u>did</u> the organization (business model) viably work?
➤ PRESENT: How <u>does</u> the organization (business model) viably work *especially to viably eliminate pain of X*?
➤ FUTURE: How <u>will</u> the organization (business model) viably work *especially to viably eliminate pain of X*?

In contrast, the five-step design process deals only with one question and time frame:

FUTURE: How <u>will</u> the organization (business model) viably work?

It is important to note that the Business Model Generation book does not explicitly focus on answering a **Pain Solving Question (PSQ)** or a **Delight Achievement Questions (DAQ)** *such as How Might We Viably Achieve Goal (HMWVAG) of "Y"?* In the book, the questions, which are provided regarding the Business Model Canvas, relate to each of the 9 building blocks. So, many practitioners of the Business Model Canvas see the metaphorical trees but are lost in the forest; they see the details but miss the big picture of a business model innovation or performance improvement project.

One could say that the three-step process deals with both business model improvement and innovation projects while the five-step process focuses on business model innovation projects.

Three-step Generic Process for Using a Business Model Canvas
1. Plot the Canvas on a Poster
2. Put the Poster on the Wall
3. Sketch out Your Business Model

The Three-step Generic Process assumes that the practitioner knows the Pain Solving Question and has relevant information. The process may therefore be geared towards an organization with an existing business model. In that case, a high level purpose of the Business Model Canvas may be to answer the question: *Who are we?*

A strategic purpose of using the Business Model Canvas may be to have a team develop a shared understanding of as well as a common textual and visual language for describing an organization's existing business model. Such a baseline Business Model Canvas is needed especially for business model improvement projects and business model disruptive innovation ("blue ocean") projects.

A fully populated Business Model Canvas of an ongoing (profitable) business should transparently and visually describe how the business creates, delivers, and capture value (profit) while reducing the pain of its most important customer. In short, the canvas should describe a **"proven" or "done" business model solution at a given point in time**. Nevertheless, a *proven Business Model Canvas* of an existing organization is a living document. Consequently, the existing Business Model (Canvas) should be checked in real-time to see whether ongoing projects and initiatives support or detract the documented business model from achieving its stated strategy and explicit goal of reducing a validated pain.

Without a stated Pain Solving Question (PSQ), strategy, or goal for a business model or a Delight Achievement Question (DAQ), use of a Business Model Canvas is reduced to a 'scorecard' of apparently discrete building blocks. Instead of the Canvas being used as a tool for managing competitive strategy and improving business performance and profit, the Business Model Canvas becomes a form to be randomly completed or at worst, a visual checklist.

For a startup, which does not yet have a proven or validated business model, a fully populated Business Model Canvas would refer to content of a hypothetical business model. A *hypothetical Business Model Canvas* transparently and visually describes how a business **intends to** create, deliver, and capture value (profit) as well as solve pain. Eventually, each hypothesis in a building block would have to be field tested and subsequently validated or rejected. Such a case deals with a **"planned" or "to-do" business model**. However, without a defined customer problem, pain, or strategy, populating a hypothetical Business Model Canvas may be ineffective and wasteful. In short, the Business Model Canvas of startups should be *pain-centered* especially regarding customers and important stakeholders.

Five-step Design Process for Using a Business Model Canvas
1. Mobilize: *Prepare for a successful business model design project*
2. Understand: *Research and analyze elements needed for the business model design effort*
3. Design: *Generate and test viable business model options and select the best*
4. Implement: *Implement the business model prototype in the field*
5. Manage: *Adapt and modify the business model in response to market reaction*

In the Business Model Generation book, the five-step design process is referred to as the "Business Model Design Process." The four "pain-solving" goals or 'Jobs To Get Done' for the Business Model Design Process are as follows:

EXISTING MARKET
1. **Satisfy** a *validated* unmet need (demand) or eliminate pain in existing market *("Red Ocean" business model)*

HYBRID (TWO/MULTI-SIDED) MARKET
2. **Disrupt** or inexpensively eliminate pain in an existing market with underserved and/or overserved customers; non-customers *("Disruptive" business model)*

NEW MARKET
3. **Create or invent** *innovative product, service, or technology* to radically reduce pain and increase delight for underserved customers and non-customers *("Blue Ocean" business model)*
4. **Create or invent** a *pipe/platform business model* for a new Job To Get Done, new market, or new Pain-To-Be-Solved *("Blue Ocean" business model)*

As in the case of the three-step generic process, the five-step design process lacks an overarching Pain Solving Question (PSQ) or Delight Achievement Question (DAQ). Such a question would create greater clarity, motivation, and focus for using the Business Model Canvas. An alternative overarching question for using a Business Model Canvas is a **Pain Solving Question (PSQ)**. The formal structure of a Pain Solving Question is as follows:
How Might We Eliminate Pain (HMWEP) of "X"?

"X" represents any object; it's recommended however that initially X should refer to a targeted customer segment (who want a certain job to get done but are encountering obstacles).

Mobilize, the first step of the Business Model Design Process, can be directly related to an individual, a team, or an organization

formulating a Pain Solving Question. The rest of the steps –
Understand, Design, Implement, and Manage – can be regarded
as activities for continuously answering the Pain Solving
Question. Consequently, the Business Model Design Process can
be reduced to a Question-and-Answer process as follows:

PAIN SOLVING QUESTION (PSQ)
1. Mobilize **(Question)**: *Prepare for a successful business model design project*

ITERATIVE ANSWER (IA)
2. Understand **(Pain)**: *Research and analyze elements needed for the business model design effort*
3. Design **(Plan)**: *Generate and test viable business model options and select the best*
4. Implement **(Do)**: *Implement the business model prototype in the field*
5. Manage **(Review)**: *Adapt and modify the business model in response to market reaction*

The process described above especially in steps 2, 3, 4, and 5
above is tied to the Pain-Plan-Do-Review (PPDR) Cycle for
facilitating pain solving and learning. The five topics or "fingers"
of Question; Pain; Plan; Do; Review constitute the elements of
the **Community Happiness Canvas**, which is a tool that I
developed for facilitating Open & Multilevel Pain Solving
(OMPS). A fun way to illustrate the five topics or fingers of the
Community Happiness Canvas is to use a "Hand Map."

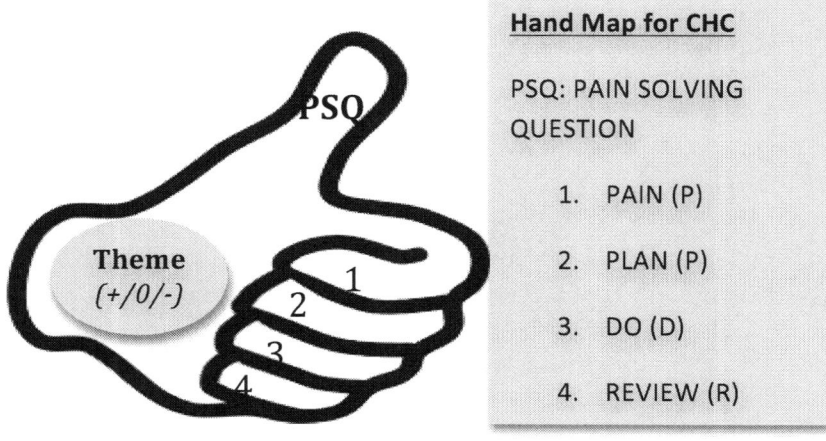

Hand Map for CHC

PSQ: PAIN SOLVING QUESTION

1. PAIN (P)

2. PLAN (P)

3. DO (D)

4. REVIEW (R)

The topics of the Community Happiness Canvas (CHC) exist in a multilevel hierarchy. The visual template for the first level may be referred to as a **"boxing glove"** because of its dual structure: thumb and rest of fingers. More specifically, the first level has a two-part structure in the form of a question-and-answer: Pain Solving Question (PSQ) and Pain-Plan-Do-Review (PPDR) Cycle.

The second level is more granular and has five "fingers" or topics. The visual template for the second level is called a **Hand Map.** The structure of a Hand Map is like in a Mind Map: the central topic in the palm of the hand while *each finger corresponds to a branch or "basic ordering idea" of a Mind Map.* There are two main differences between a Mind Map and Hand Map. First, the classic Hand Map has a maximum of five fingers or basic ordering idea. Second, each finger has a fixed description: **Thumb** (Pain Solving Question); **First Finger** (Pain); **Second Finger** (Plan); **Third Finger** (Do); **Fourth Finger** (Review). Consequently, every pain solving method can be mapped on to the five fingers of a hand. Such mapping accelerates learning. The Hand Map below illustrates the "five fingers" of the Business Model Design Process that was earlier described.

Hand Map *("Five Fingers")* for Business Model Design Process

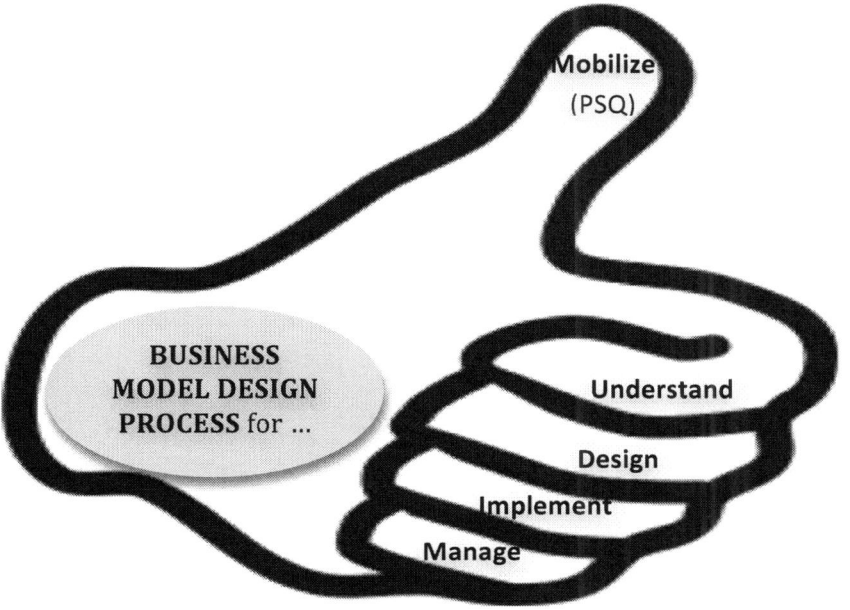

Relating the five steps of the Business Model Design Process to the Hand Map and consequently to the Community Happiness Canvas reveals that four types of Business Model Canvas must be used in a business model design project. At best, each step of the Pain-Plan-Do-Review (PPDR) Cycle requires its business model map. Here is a *family of Business Model Canvas* for the Business Model Design Process:

1. **Pain-Business Model Canvas**: *Understand* (Empathize; Define)
2. **Plan-Business Model Canvas:** *Design* (Ideate)
3. **Do-Business Model Canvas:** *Implement* (Prototype; Test)
4. **Review-Business Model Canvas:** *Manage* (Reflect)

The third level of the Community Happiness Canvas is shown below.

Hierarchical Outline for Community Happiness Canvas (CHC)

	Community Happiness Canvas: Topics *(Pain-Plan-Do-Review (PPDR) Cycle; Ecosystem)*
	PAIN SOLVING QUESTION (PSQ): *How Might We Eliminate Pain (HMWEP) of "X"?* **1. PAIN** (Collect; *Empathize; Define*) 1.1 **Problem/Challenge/Pain** 1.2 Customers/Stakeholders 1.3 **Other Solutions** **2. PLAN** (To Do: **Ideas**; *Ideate*) 2.1 Proposed Solution (End) 2.2 Plan of Action (Ways) 2.3 Resources (Means) **3. DO** (Doing: **Build/ Prototype; Measure; *Test*)** **4. REVIEW** (Done: **Learn**; Innovation Accounting) 4.1 Budget: COST (STRUCTURE) 4.2 Motivation: BENEFITS – REVENUE (STREAMS)

It is important to note that the second level of the Community Happiness Canvas is process-driven and based on the Pain-Plan-Do-Review (PPDR) Cycle. In contrast, the third level focuses on the elements or building blocks of a project, organization, business model, or ecosystem. Consequently, the Community Happiness Canvas can be considered as a "SpaceTime" template that seamlessly integrates the process of pain solving and project management with the elements of a project, system business model, or an organization.

The graphic below shows correspondences between the five-step design process and elements of the Community Happiness Canvas. Similar topics on each side of the table can be exchanged.

Bus. Model Design Process vs. Community Happiness Canvas

Business Model Design Process: Topics/Questions (*Elements of Extended Enterprise/ System*)	Community Happiness Canvas: Topics (*Pain-Plan-Do-Review (PPDR) Cycle; Ecosystem*)
Five-Step Business Model Design 1. **Mobilize** 2. **Understand** 3. **Design** 4. **Implement** 5. **Manage**	**PAIN SOLVING QUESTION (PSQ):** *How Might We Eliminate Pain (HMWEP) of "X"?* **1. PAIN** (Collect; *Empathize; Define*) 1.1 **Problem/Challenge/Pain** 1.2 Customers/Stakeholders 1.3 **Other Solutions** **2. PLAN** (To Do: **Ideas**; *Ideate*) 2.1 Proposed Solution (End) 2.2 Plan of Action (Ways) 2.3 Resources (Means) **3. DO** (Doing: **Build/ Prototype**; **Measure**; *Test*) **4. REVIEW** (Done: **Learn**; Innovation Accounting) 4.1 Budget: COST (STRUCTURE) 4.2 Motivation: BENEFITS – REVENUE (STREAMS)

Using the logic of the Community Happiness Canvas methodology, we can prepare a graphic that seamlessly integrates the Business Model Design Process Canvas with the building blocks of the Business Model Canvas and Community Happiness Canvas. The graphic is presented below.

Business Model Design Process for Business Model Canvas

Business Model Canvas: Topics/Questions *(Elements of Extended Enterprise/ System)*	**Community Happiness Canvas/Business Model Design Process:** Topics *(Pain-Plan-Do-Review (PPDR) Cycle; Ecosystem)*
1. **Customer Segments** (CS) 2. **Customer Relationships** (CR) 3. **Channels** (CH) 4. **Key Partners** (KP) 5. **Value Proposition** (VP) 6. **Key Activities** (KA) 7. **Key Resources** (KR) 8. **Cost Structure** (C$) 9. **Revenue Streams** (R$)	MOBILIZE **(PSQ):** *How Might We Eliminate Pain (HMWEP) of "X"?* 1. UNDERSTAND (Collect; *Empathize; Define*) 1.1 **Problem/Challenge/Pain** 1.2 Customers/Stakeholders 1.3 **Other Solutions** 2. DESIGN (To Do: **Ideas;** *Ideate*) 2.1 Proposed Solution (End) 2.2 Plan of Action (Ways) 2.3 Resources (Means) 3. IMPLEMENT (Doing: **Build/ Prototype; Measure;** *Test*) 4. MANAGE (Done: **Learn;** Innovation Accounting) 4.1 Budget: COST (STRUCTURE) 4.2 Motivation: BENEFITS – REVENUE (STREAMS)

An advantage of the above table is that it presents one source for learning about the building blocks of the Business Model Canvas as well as a systematic process for solving pain using the Canvas.

Another advantage of the table is that the framework is a platform for pain solving tools and methodologies. So, a variety of business tools can be mixed and matched with those of the Business Model Canvas methodology. The question-and-answer structure of the five fingers as well as the hierarchical outline of the Community Happiness Canvas can directly be mapped to the every methodology and tool for pain solving and project management.

The table explicitly incorporates ideas from tools such in Design Thinking, Lean Startup Method, Kanban Board, GTD System, Cost Benefit Analysis, and Project Management. The table can be used not only with the building blocks of the Business Model Canvas but also with its derivative Canvases such as in the Mission Model Canvas, Value Proposition Canvas, Mission Model Canvas, Personal Business Model Canvas, and Lean Canvas. The table therefore forms the foundation of a universal language for the emerging domain of Business Model Project Management.

In the spirit of a universal language for business modeling, a Business Model Canvas is presented with a "fixed" reference number for each building block. Although the numbers can refer to any object, they generally refer to topics of the Business Model Canvas as well as reflect the flow of the Business Model Design Process and pain solving. The numbers can also be categorized as shown below.

Value Creator Chain/Loop & Reference Number System for Building Blocks in Business Modeling Using a Micro-Canvas

VALUE CREATOR		OUTPUT	VALUE RECIPIENT	
4	6	5	2	1
	7		3	
8		9 FEEDBACK: Impacts (-/+)		

6 THE LEANEST BUSINESS MODEL CANVAS: "ONE PAGE BUSINESS PLAN" VS. "ONE LINE BUSINESS PLAN"

What is the "leanest" Business Model Canvas in the world today?

To effectively answer the above question, we must consider its two dimensions as sub-questions:

- *What is the "leanest" number of topics for the Business Model Canvas?*

- *What is the "leanest" graphic layout for the Business Model Canvas?*

By definition, the number of business modeling topics on a Business Model Canvas is 9. Its business modeling topics are listed below:

1. Customer Segments (CS)
2. Customer Relationships (CR)
3. Channels (CH)
4. Key Partners (KP)
5. Value Proposition (VP)
6. Key Activities (KA)
7. Key Resources (KR)
8. Cost Structure (C$)
9. Revenue Streams (R$)

All "internal" derivatives of the Business Model Canvas by Osterwalder et al such as the Mission Model Canvas and Personal Business Model Canvas have 9 business modeling topics. The Value Proposition Canvas, which is derived from the Business Model Canvas, has two business modeling topics: Value Map (Value Proposition) and Customer Profile (Customer Segment). Each of the aforementioned topics, however, has sub-topics that refer to trade-off. For the Value Map, trade-off of products and services is described in terms of "Pain Relievers" and "Gain Creators." The Customer Profile describes trade-off of customer segment in terms of "Pains" and "Gains." Note that *Value Map does not describe "Functionality."*

The majority of "external derivatives" of the Business Model Canvas such as the Lean Canvas uses 9 business modeling topics. Not-for-Profit canvases especially for the social sector tend to use more than 9 business modeling topics as they include topics for mission, social costs, and social benefits. Although the meso-canvas uses four categories of topics, the classic Business Model Canvas uses 9 topics. All business model diagrams with 8 or more business modeling topics are described as "fat;" the majority of people struggle to hold more than 7 objects in their working memory.

A *"Fat"* Business Model Canvas is presented below.

"Fat" **Business Model Canvas** (9 topics; 9 building blocks)

KP	KA	VP	CR	CS
	KR		CH	

C$	R$

But, what is the minimum number of topics that is required to describe a business model as well as fully answer a Pain Solving Question (PSQ)? Based on the existing literature on business modeling, the minimum number of business modeling topics is four. Typically, four question-tags are used to describe the minimum business model or story:

- o Who
- o What
- o How
- o Why

Incidentally, the four question-tags above correspond to the four categories that Osterwalder uses in his meso-canvas to describe a business model:

- o Who: **Customer** (CS; CR; CH)
- o What: **Offer** (VP)
- o How: **Infrastructure** (KA; KR; KP)
- o Why: **Finance** (C$; R$)

We shall now explore the second sub-question of:
- ▪ *What is the "leanest" graphic layout for the Business Model Canvas?*

In geometry, there are four types of structures: point (zero dimension); line (one dimension); plane (two dimensions); solid (three dimensions). The classic presentation of the Business Model Canvas is as a tessellated block in 2D. In the Business Model Generation book, there is a graphic in which the Business Model Canvas is presented in 3D; a 3D video animation also exists online. There is a horizontal list of 9 business modeling topics in the Business Model Generation book. One can regard that list of Osterwalder's 9 business modeling topics as a linear Business Model Canvas. However, the logic behind the sequence of topics is not clear.

In my research on system models, I've discovered that a "directed" line with 4 nodes is the "leanest" shape for describing ANY viable or living organization, system, communication, story, business idea, mission/vision statement, strategy, or business model. A "strip" is what I call such a directed line. A strip without annotation is shown below.

Strip (4 Nodes of Value Creator Chain, Story, System, or <u>Transaction Map</u>)

The big question is: Can a "strip" be used to present the 4 main categories of business modeling topics as well as the 9 business modeling topics of the Business Model Canvas? The answer is, "Yes!" Shown below are two types of "Business Model Strips." The order of the categories matters and has greater significance especially when each category is placed adjacent to each "node." This Business Model Strip can instantly be drawn ANYWHERE..

Lean **Business Model Canvas Strip** ('StorySpine' of 4 Nodes/Categories)

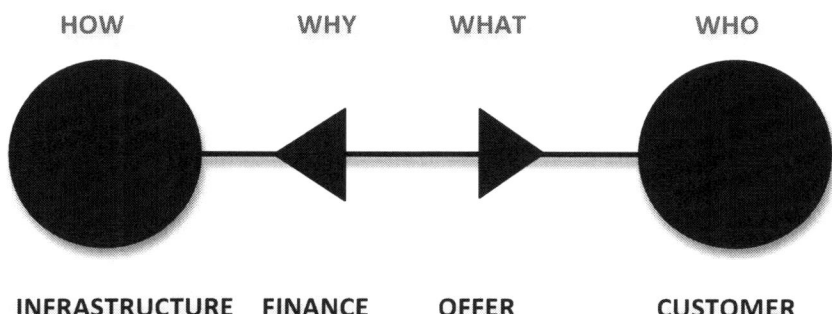

Lean **Business Model Canvas Strip** ('StorySpine' Illustrating 4 Business Modeling Nodes/Categories & 9 Business Modeling Topics)

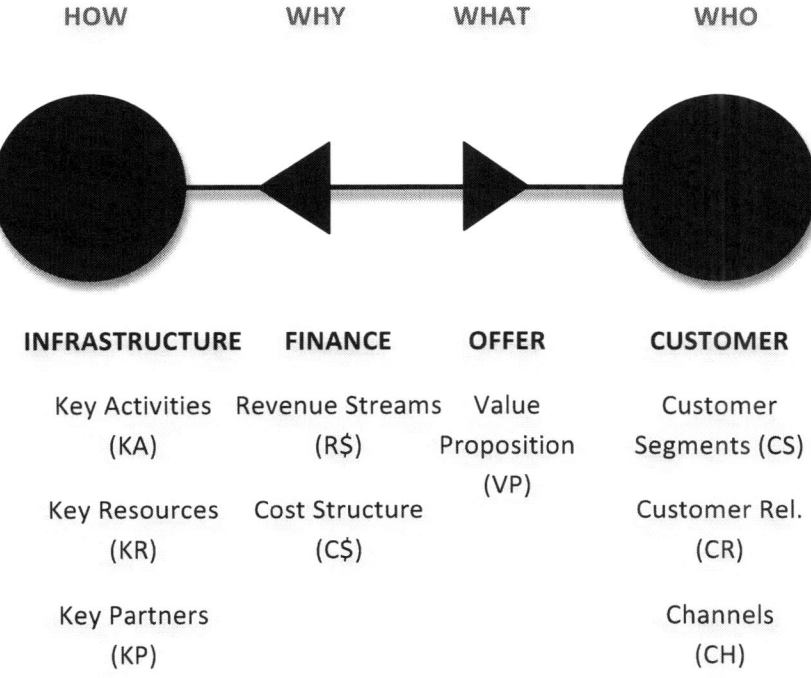

HOW	WHY	WHAT	WHO
INFRASTRUCTURE	**FINANCE**	**OFFER**	**CUSTOMER**
Key Activities (KA)	Revenue Streams (R$)	Value Proposition (VP)	Customer Segments (CS)
Key Resources (KR)	Cost Structure (C$)		Customer Rel. (CR)
Key Partners (KP)			Channels (CH)

A leaner way to present a Business Model Strip using the 9 topics from the Business Model Canvas is to use abbreviations as follows:

Leaner **Business Model Canvas Strip** ('StorySpine')

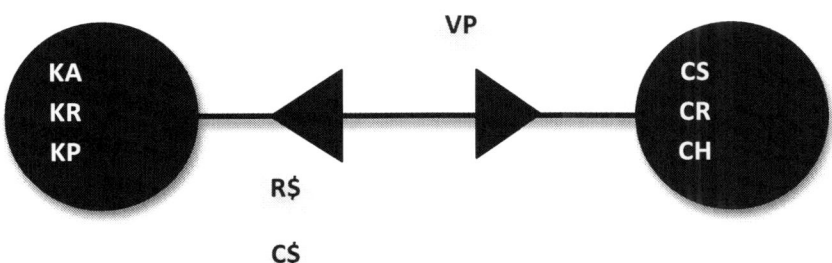

If we use the descriptors of "Value Creator" and "Value Recipient," we can present the leanest Business Model Canvas Strip. A Value Creator (VC) is an individual, team, or organization that creates, delivers, and captures/shares value. In contrast, the Value Recipient (VR) receives or experiences the value and in return provides feedback which may be tangible (cash) and/or intangible (information). The Strip is *human-centered* and consequently focuses on interactions, flows, and exchanges. The "exchange nodes" or triangles include P.I.G.S. (Product; Information; Goods; Service). Each of the four nodes includes trade-off (delight; pain). Theoretically, a "channel" exists between any two nodes in a flow.

Leanest **Business Model Canvas Strip:** *"One Line Business Model (OLBM)"*

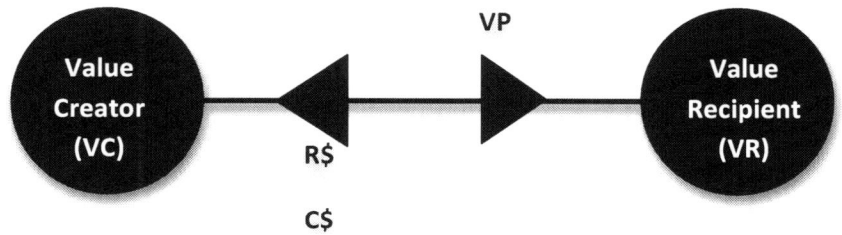

The **syntax, one-sentence story, plot, storyline, or headline** of the "Leanest Business Model Canvas Strip" is as follows:

[Value Creator] offers [Value Proposition] to [Value Recipient] who accepts and/or experiences it while providing [Feedback] to [Value Creator].

The above one-sentence, mini-story, plot, or headline can then be expanded by zooming into the content of the nodes: Value Recipient, Value Proposition, Feedback, and Value Creator. By especially using the "chunks" of Value Recipient (VR) and Value Creator (VC), narration of a business model story is greatly simplified and understood as well as instantly presented. With the above strip, the big picture is first painted before painting the small picture or details. This contrasts the approach of storytelling using the classic Business Model Canvas, where there is often cognitive overload information in all of the 9 building blocks.

It is important to note that the above story can be described as having a "Respond-and-Sense" or "Value Creator-led" or "Supply Chain" syntax. One can also develop a one-sentence story that has a "Sense-and-Respond" or "Value Recipient-led" syntax. The latter mini-story is more customer-focused. Here is an example of the plot of a customer-focused or "pull" story. Innovation based on actual *pull stories* are more efficient with respect to use of organizational resources than *push stories*.

<u>Sense-and-Respond ("Pull") Storyline: *How Might We Eliminate Pain of X?*</u>

[Value Recipient] provides [Feedback/Signal/Cue] to [Value Creator] who offers [Value Proposition] to [Value Recipient].

To illustrate similarities and differences between the visual template of a Business Model Canvas and a Business Model Canvas Strip, an example follows. The example relates to the business model for Apple's classic iPod.

Lean Business Model Canvas (BMC) for Apple's Classic iPod
PSQ: *How Might We Eliminate Pain (HMWEP) of [High-end Music Lover]?*

KP	KA	VP ▶O	CR	CS
Original Equipment Manufacturers (OEM)/ Record Companies	Hardware Design/ Software Design/ Marketing & Sales/ Branding/ Outsourcing	*"A Thousand Songs in Your Pocket"* (iPod)	Customer Intimacy: Face-to-face Customer Service & Support	High-end music lover
VC	**KR** Staff/ Brand/ iTunes Software/ iPod Hardware/ Contracts/ Infra-structure		**CH** Retailers/ Apple Stores/ Apple.com	**VR**

C$	R$
Staff/Manufacturing/Marketing, Advertising & Sales/Branding/ Infrastructure **F**	Asset (Product) Sale

A similar *Lean* Business Model Canvas for Apple's iPod can be found in the Business Model Generation book.

Here is a Business Model Canvas Strip for Apple's iPod.

Business Model Canvas (BMC) Strip for Apple's Classic iPod
PSQ: *How Might We Eliminate Pain (HMWEP) of [High-end Music Lover]?*

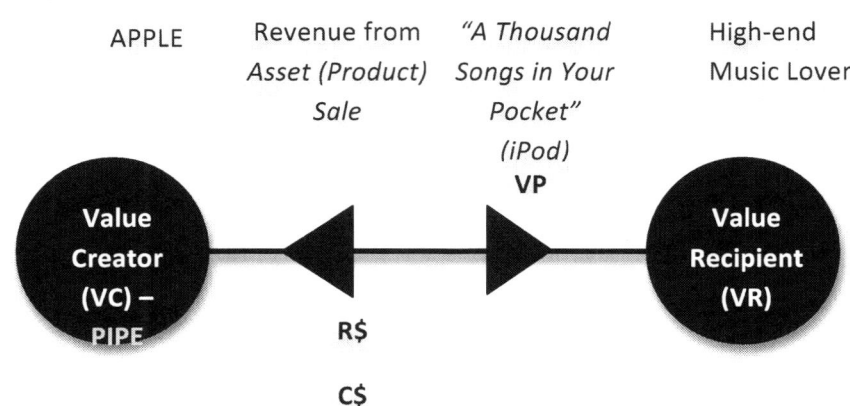

From the above BMC Strip, on can write the following Respond-and-Sense Story Plot or Headline. Note that the plot is *delight and not pain-focused*.

APPLE offers **"A Thousand Songs in Your Pocket"** to **High-end Music Lover** who accepts and/or experiences it while providing **Money** to **APPLE**.

As noted earlier, a node can be chosen and expanded upon especially using the framework of the Value Proposition Canvas which focuses on the nodes of "Value Recipient (VR)" and "Value Proposition (VP)." The Value Proposition Canvas is not the only tool, its topics of which can be directly layered on the BMC Strip. In my experience, the topic of every pain solving tool can easily be layered on the Strip because of its linear visual structure. The Strip also inherently portrays a loop or circular cause-effect structure.

The classic Business Model Canvas is sometimes (erroneously) positioned and referred to as a **"One Page Business Plan."** Although not factually accurate, a Business Model Canvas Strip can be referred to as a **"One Line Business Plan."** In theory, a One Line Business Plan should answer at least two questions: What is the present business model of the organization? What is the future business model of the organization? Using the Business Model Strip, one can quickly show the two-states of a business model as two rows of blocks that are aligned with the four nodes of a Strip. Such a comparative illustration is very useful when crafting and managing a *Blue Ocean or Disruptive Innovation Strategy (Business model)*.

The previous paragraph contains a description of how the Business Model Canvas Strip can be used to illustrate two "lines of business models" when preparing a business plan. One **Line of Business Model (LBM)** could be for a Red Ocean Business Model while the other LBM could be for a Blue Ocean Business Model. Nevertheless, a page containing a line diagram of a Business Model Canvas Strip can contain or present several *textual* Lines of Business Models such as in the case for platforms: two-sided markets; multi-sided markets.

There are many visual variations for presenting a Business Model Strip as a pipe business model (single market) or platform business model (two or multi-sided markets). A Business Model Strip can have a horizontal, vertical, or oblique orientation. Also, a line diagram of a Business Model Strip can have several groups of textual information, each group of which describes a *Line of Business Model.*

Below is an archetypal visual representation of a Business Model Strip that can be used for instantly prototyping, designing, or presenting the business model platform of a two/three-sided market. Examples of a two-sided market include a *school, freemium, and traditional brokerage model.* Organizations with multi-sided markets include *Apple, Google, Microsoft, Uber, and Airbnb.* Every **non-profit organization** has a platform business model.

Business Model Strip (BMS) Platform: Two/Three-sided Market (External/Cross-Network Effects are Not Illustrated)

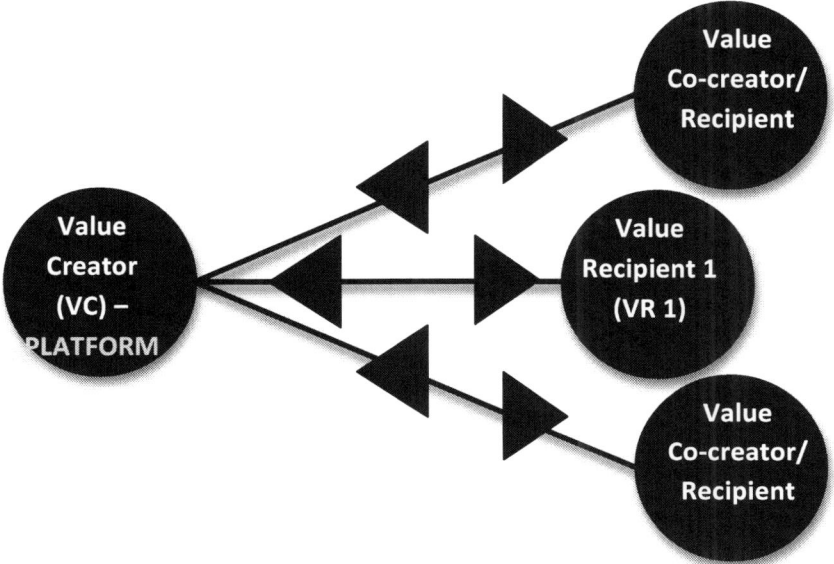

As an example, the Business Model StripPlatform of the Business Model Generation book project is presented below.

Business Model Strip (BMS) Platform for *Business Model Generation* **Book Project - 2009:** Multi-sided Market *(Channels/Customer Relationships as well as Links or Network Effects Between Recipients are Omitted for Clarity)*

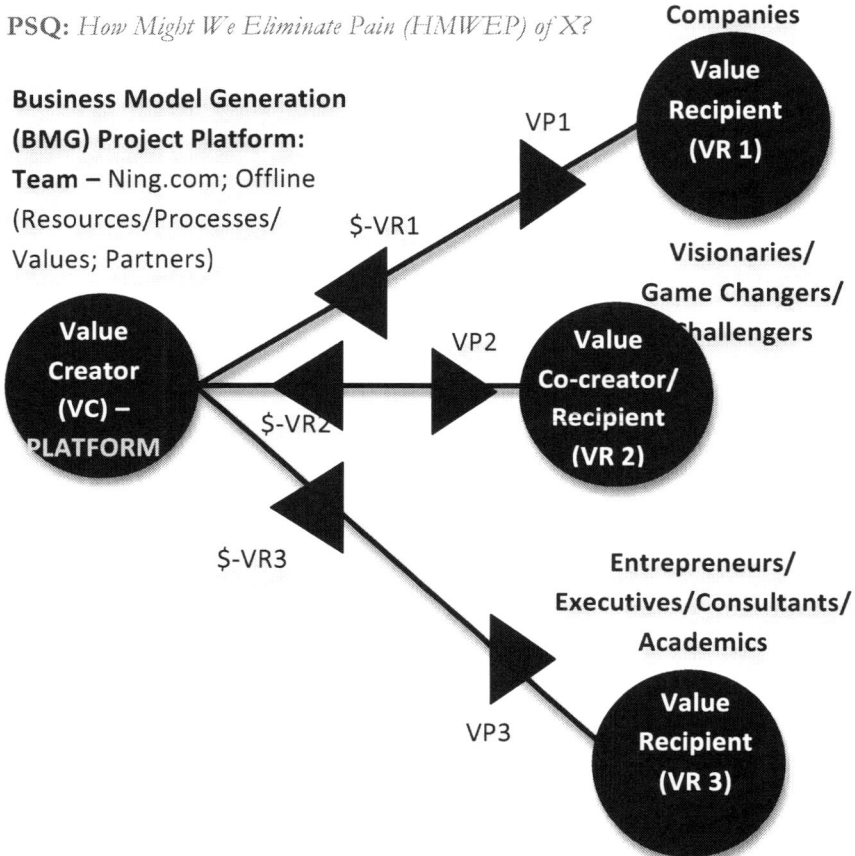

Value Recipient (VR)	Feedback (F): Revenue Stream	Output (O); Offer: Value Proposition (VP)
VR1: Companies	$-VR1: *Fee*	VP1: *Customized Book*
VR2: Visionaries/Game Changers/Challengers	$-VR2: *Pre-order/ Hub Member Fee*	VP2: *Co-creation of a potential bestseller*
VR3: Entrepreneurs/ Execs/Consultants/…	$-VR3: *Book sale: Royalties (from Publisher)*	VP3: *Visual, practical, and beautiful book for business model innovators*

A discussion of the relationship between the Business Model Canvas and Business Model Strip would not be complete without mentioning the Value Proposition Canvas. In their book, "Value Proposition Design," Osterwalder et al note that the purpose of the Value Proposition Canvas is "to Design and Test great value propositions in an iterative search for what customers want." Their visual tool of the Value Proposition Canvas focuses on two building blocks of the Business Model Canvas: "Value Proposition (VP)" and "Customer Segments (CS)." In the language of the Business Model Strip, the Value Proposition Canvas respectively focuses on the "Output (O)" and "Value Recipient (VR)." The diagram below shows the building blocks of the Value Proposition Canvas within the context of the Business Model Strip. For any Value Creator, *fitness or synergy* between the Product Value Map and Customer Profile should continuously be checked. Unlike in the Value Proposition Canvas, the diagram below explicitly focuses on the concept of product trade-off as well as customer trade-off.

Business Model Strip Using Symbols as in the Value Proposition Canvas

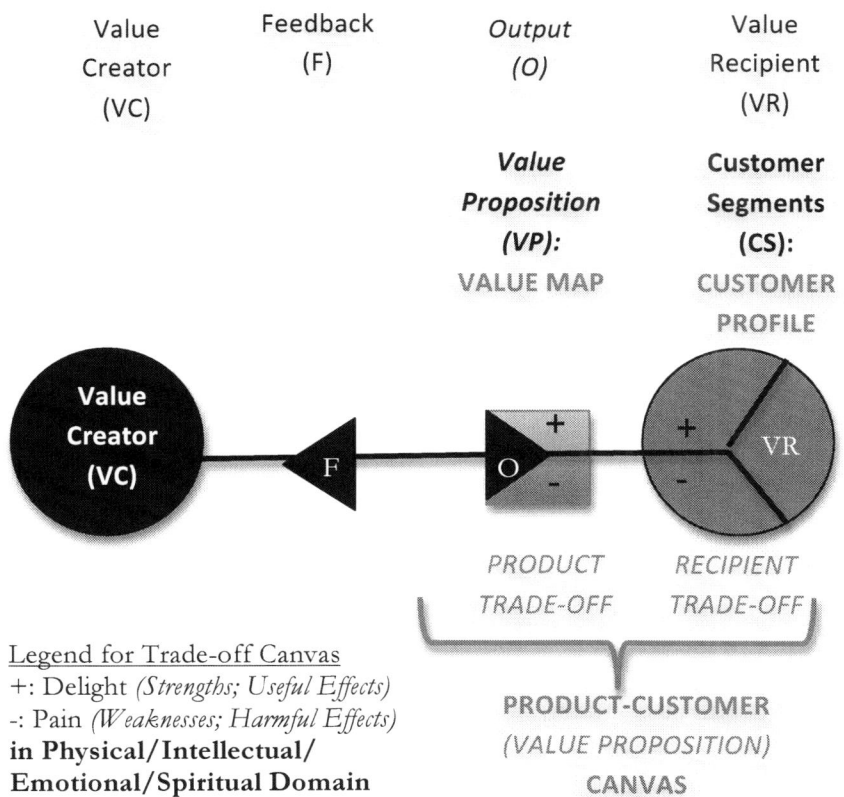

Legend for Trade-off Canvas
+: Delight *(Strengths; Useful Effects)*
-: Pain *(Weaknesses; Harmful Effects)*
**in Physical/Intellectual/
Emotional/Spiritual Domain**

Here is a Business Model Strip-Trade-off Canvas for Apple's Classic iPod

Business Model Strip Using Symbols as in the Value Proposition for Apple's Classic iPod

PSQ: *How Might We Eliminate Pain (HMWEP) of [High-end Music Lover]?*

Business Model Strip Using Symbols as in the Value Proposition Canvas

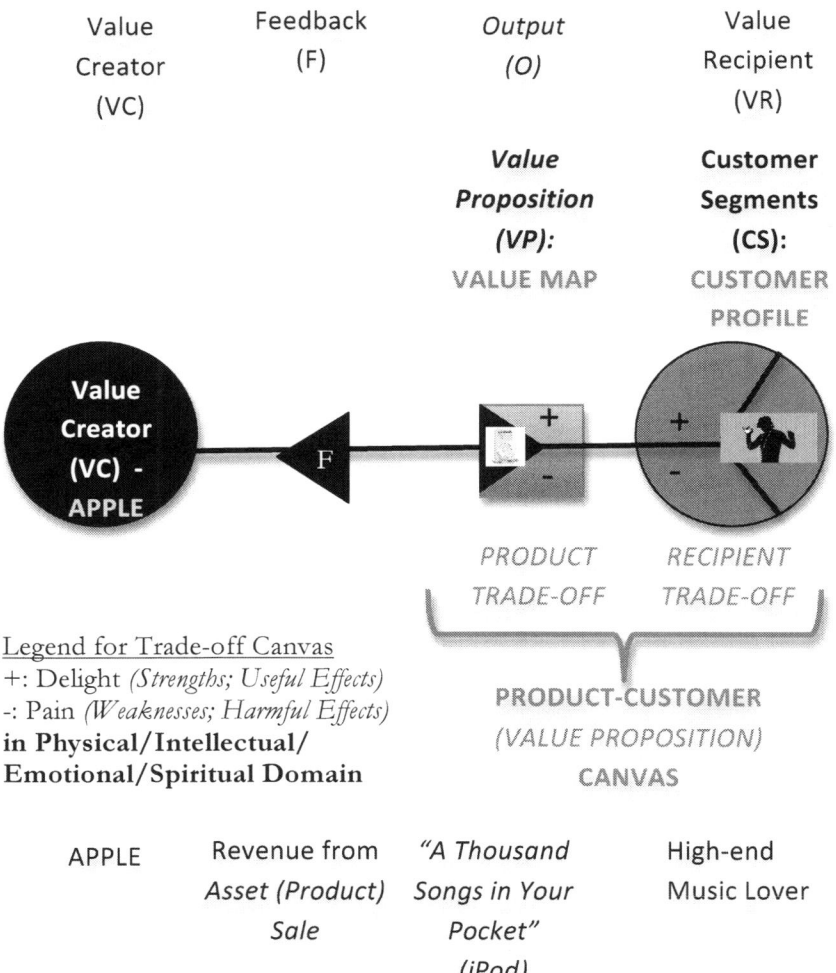

Value Creator (VC)	Feedback (F)	Output (O)	Value Recipient (VR)
		Value Proposition (VP): VALUE MAP	**Customer Segments (CS):** CUSTOMER PROFILE

PRODUCT TRADE-OFF   RECIPIENT TRADE-OFF

PRODUCT-CUSTOMER
(VALUE PROPOSITION)
CANVAS

Legend for Trade-off Canvas
+: Delight *(Strengths; Useful Effects)*
-: Pain *(Weaknesses; Harmful Effects)*
in Physical/Intellectual/
Emotional/Spiritual Domain

APPLE	Revenue from Asset (Product) Sale	"A Thousand Songs in Your Pocket" (iPod)	High-end Music Lover

7 WHAT IS THE IDEAL BUSINESS MODELING TOOL FOR ANSWERING A PAIN SOLVING QUESTION?

In the literature on visual business modeling and in particular, **visual descriptions of how an organization works, transacts business, or makes profit while resolving pain**, the topics or elements of a business model are presented using four types of visual tools:

- **Fat ("Block") Business Modeling Tools:** Block Diagram; Grid; TreeMap; Rectangular Tessellation; Non-rectangular Tessellation; 3D-Tunnel Tessellation; House; Picture Frame; Tennis Court; (Monopoly) Gameboard; Jigsaw; Table; Affinity Diagram;

Examples: *Business Model Canvas; Mission Model Canvas; Personal Business Model Canvas; Lean Canvas; SEMPORCES Fractal Grid; Multiscreen Diagram; Value Chain; Business Model Innovation (Magic) Triangle; Business Model Affinity Diagram; Unified Business Model Framework; Business Ecosystem Framework*

- **Lean ("Single Line") Business Modeling Tools:** Linear List; Line Diagram (Directed; Undirected); Chain; Timeline (Straight; Circular); Curve; "Dumbbell" Diagram; Arrow of Time

Examples: *Supply Chain; SIPOC Diagram; Business Model Strip; SEMPORCES Chain; Design-Needs-Aspiration (DNA) Model; List of Innovate Salone Topics (LIST); Six Pain Solving Actors; Investment Meter*

- **Hybrid ("Hierarchy; Network") Business Modeling Tools:** Tree Hierarchy; Mind Map; Cycle; Loop; Network Diagram; Activity Chart; Concept Diagram; Semantic Net; Process Diagram; (Baseball) Diamond; Carbon Molecule; Center-Periphery Diagram;

Examples: *Business Model Template; Organizational Chart; Organigram; SIPOC Diagram; SEMPORCES Mind Map; e-Business Model Schematic; Value Net; Balanced Scorecard; Strategy Map; Value Network; Input-Processing-Output-Feedback (IPOF) Diagram; 4 Box Business Model; 7C's Business Model; Shared Value Map*

- **Punctiform ("Point") Business Modeling Tools:** Profitability Point; Value (Benefit/Cost) Point; ROI; Performance Scorecard

Examples: *Value Engine Map; Financial Options Tree; Project Outcome Story Tree (POST); "Pirate" Metrics; Balanced Scorecard; Value Curve; Strategy Canvas*

In the Business Model Generation book, there is no example of a Punctiform (Point) Business Modeling Diagram. There are only examples on the three other diagrams. However, there is one Lean (Single Line) Business Modeling Diagram which consists of an annotated list of the 9 building blocks. The only hybrid diagram in the book presents an example of the Business Model Template that is applied to illustrate the business model of a fictitious company called "SuperToast." Over 95% of the business model presentations in the book use the Business Model Canvas.

Given the universe of existing diagrams for visual business modeling, *what is the "Ideal Business Modeling (IBM)" tool for answering a Pain Solving Question (PSQ)?* **But first, what is Ideal Business Modeling (IBM)?**

The concept of Ideal Business Modeling is influenced by the idea of the Ideal Final Result (IFR) in TRIZ methodology. "TRIZ" is a Russian acronym for "Theory of Inventive Problem Solving." Based on TRIZ, the **Ideal Final Result for a project goal or Job To Get Done describes a stakeholder's outcome, result, or solution with zero pain and infinite delight which is instantly produced on demand in any place using freely available or no additional resources and at (virtually) zero cost.** In short, the Ideal Final Result has zero trade-off or infinite value.

Although the Ideal Final Result is a utopic idea, many people have observed that products, organizations, and systems broadly evolve towards the Ideal Final Result. Otherwise, they perish or eventually die. This may be called the "Law of Ideal Final Result (IFR)." The Law of IFR is very powerful as it has both explanatory and predictive powers regarding the evolution of products, organizations, systems, and business models. In this book, we replace the term of IFR with "Ideal Value Proposition (IVP)."

In the domain of business modeling, we can say that an Ideal Business Modeling (IBM) tool delivers an Ideal Value Proposition (IVP) for a Pain Solving Question. Below are 7 features of the Ideal Value Proposition tool.
IVP: "North Star" for Answering a Pain Solving Question (PSQ)
- Goal or Job To Get Done: *Visually document, organize, manage, and evaluate whole and parts of business models, organizations, projects and systems*
- Outcome, Result, or Experience: *Physical; Intellectual; Emotional; Spiritual; Total (Immersive)*
- Pain (-) including Size, Cost, Complexity, and Inconvenience: *Zero*
- Delight (+) including Performance, Quality, and "Play": *Infinite*
- Trade-off (-/+): *Zero;* Value (+/-): *Infinite (Happiness)*
- Delivery Time: *Instantly; Zero; On Demand; Just In Time*
- Location: *Anywhere; Everywhere*

In order to rapidly organize and evaluate visual business modeling tools vis-à-vis the Ideal Value Proposition, we can use a **Value Engine Map**, a template of which is produced below. The horizontal axis of the Value Engine Map deals with Pain while the vertical axis deals with Delight. The Value Engine Map also features the Ideal Value Proposition which has zero pain and infinite delight. Visual business modeling tools can be evaluated based on how far or near they are relative to the Ideal Value Proposition.

When the Pain axis of the Value Engine Map describes "Cost" while the Delight axis describes "Revenue," each cell or point on the map represents a business model. A Cost-Revenue Value Engine Map can therefore be described as a *Punctiform Business Modeling tool* for for-profit organizations. For non-profit organizations, a different performance indicator such as "Effectiveness" can be chosen for the Delight axis.

Value Engine Map: What is the Minimum Viable Output (MVO) for Delivering the Ideal Value Proposition (IVP)?

Time: *Past (Done)/ Present (Doing)/ Future (To Do)*
Goal or Job To Get Done: ....
Environment (Context; Location): ....

Ideal Value Proposition (IVP): *"Free, Perfect, Now"*

A Value Engine Map for selected visual business modeling tools is presented below. The Pain axis relates to *Learning Time, Complexity, and Cost* which are assumed to be correlated. The Delight axis refers to *Versatility*. The graphic indicates that the Business Model Canvas provides greater value than tools such as the traditional business plan, strategic plan, One Page Business Plan, and One Page Project Plan. However, the Business Model Strip (Pipe) is the simplest and most versatile tool for visual business modeling. Although the Business Model Strip (Platform) is more versatile than the Business Model Canvas, their learning curves are considered to be similar and in particular, *moderate*. Nevertheless, for modeling platforms especially multi-sided markets, the tool of a Business Model Strip (Platform) is significantly faster to use. than the Business Model Canvas.

Value Engine Map for Selected Visual Business Modeling Tools

Time: *Past (Done)/Present (Doing)/Future (To Do)*

Goal or Job To Get Done: *Document/Organize/Manage/Evaluate Business Models for Answering a Pain Solving Question (PSQ)*

Environment (Context; Location): *Profit Sector/Non-Profit Sector; Startups/Established Organizations; Innovation/Improvement Projects*

IVP: *Highest Versatility in No Time & at No Cost*

High	**Business Model Strip (Pipe):** One Line Project Plan	**Business Model Strip (Platform):** Shared Value Map	Classic Design Thinking
DELIGHT (+): Versatility *Moderate*	**Community Happiness Canvas**	**Business Model Canvas (& Derivatives)**	Lean Startup Method
Low	Brainstorming	One Page Business Plan One Page Project Plan	Traditional Business Plan Traditional Strategic Plan
	Low	*Moderate*	*High*

PAIN (-): Time (Learning); Complexity; Cost

So, what is the story behind the creation of the Business Model Strip?

The author of this book, Rod King, created the Business Model Strip in 2015 because he wanted a **visual business modeling tool that anyone (starting from a 3 year old Value Creator) could use to rapidly answer a Pain Solving Question (PSQ) for every domain on the planet.** He felt that the popular tool of the *Business Model Canvas is relatively complex, expensive, and time-consuming to learn and use as well as limited in scope for fully answering PSQs.*

Also, Rod King did not consider the Business Model Canvas to be efficient in application especially for community projects in the non-profit sector. Next, the *cause-and-effect logic* of the Business Model Canvas is non-obvious so that it is not clear how to effectively use or read it. Further, the Business Model Canvas is not effectively and easily integrated with business tools such as in the Balanced Scorecard, Strategy Map, SWOT Analysis, Blue Ocean Strategy, and Golden Circle. Finally, the Business Model Canvas does not "by default" indicate flow of resources between a Value Creator (Enterprise) and Value Recipient (Customer/Stakeholder; Channel). In short, the Business Model Canvas appears as a *static template*; the Canvas is a snapshot of a business model or project at a certain time.

Given the need for rapid prototyping and testing business models when answering a PSQ in a highly volatile environment such as in a lean startup, matured industry, or non-profit organization, Rod King did not consider the Business Model Canvas as an adequate tool. Moreover, the Canvas lacks scalability: *information as well as its logic becomes unwieldy when dealing with three or more stakeholders.* The Business Model Canvas is optimized for a single customer segment in a stable environment such as in an established business that has significant amount of money, energy, and time for business model improvement and innovation as well as pain solving.

An unlabeled **"living system" logic diagram** of a classic Business Model Strip is shown below. *This is a suggested "standard" basic symbol for visually representing any business model, organization, project, system, or supply chain for any pain to be resolved, job to get done, or goal to be achieved in any domain.*

Business Model Strip: Living System Logic Diagram of 4 Atoms (Nodes)

Visual "Molecular/Genomic" Structure of Every Living System or Organization

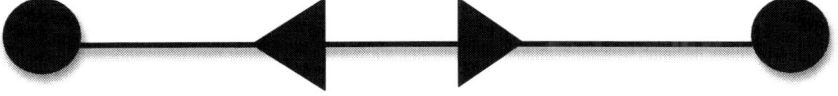

A Business Model Strip (BMS) refers to a <u>multilevel living system (MLS) map</u> that represents a "sense-and-respond feedback loop," which is involved in any transaction, trade, exchange, or interaction especially when resolving physical, intellectual (knowledge), emotional (social), and spiritual pains. Areas of application of a Business Model Strip include organizational development; business/not-for-profit projects; communication.. As a **multilevel living system map** that consists of 1 line and 4 nodes, a Business Model Strip efficiently describes how any living system, business model, organization, or project **VIABLY resolves a given pain at a given point in time**. Every business modeling tool can be mapped on to a Business Model Strip. *A Business Model Canvas is a specific and an expanded ("fat") template of a Business Model Strip.*

Each real-life node of a Business Model Strip has a trade-off: pain and delight. The ideal node has zero pain and infinite delight. The line in a Strip describes a link, conversation, or two-way communication channel.

Business Model Strip: One Line Business Model for Answering PSQ

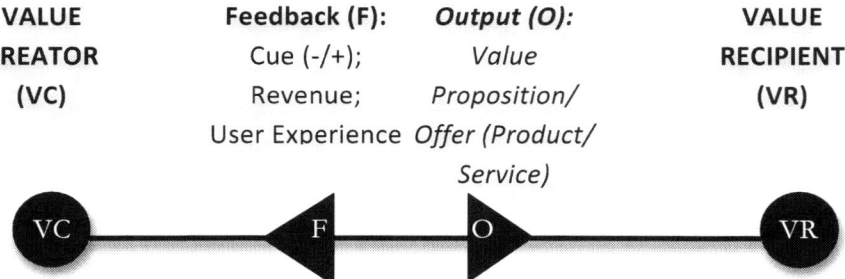

| VALUE CREATOR (VC) | Feedback (F): Cue (-/+); Revenue; User Experience | *Output (O): Value Proposition/ Offer (Product/ Service)* | VALUE RECIPIENT (VR) |

A brief description of each node of a Business Model Strip follows:
- **Value Creator (VC):** individual, team, organization, living system, provider, or "architect" that creates value or shares happiness using project resources, processes, and core values as well as partners.
  A Value Creator offers a Value Proposition (Product/Service) through channels and relationships to a Value Recipient. Two types of Value Creators exist: positive and negative Value Creators.
  A *negative Value Creator* is referred to as a *"Value Destroyer (VD)."*
- **Value Recipient (VR):** individual, team, organization, or living system that accepts and experiences the Value Proposition (Product/Service). A Value Recipient with *negative effect*, which is caused by a Value Destroyer, may be referred to as a *"Victim. (V)"*
  The Value Recipient may offer P.I.G.S. to the Value Creator. The acronym P.I.G.S. stands for Product; Information; Goods; Service.

- **Output (O):** direct outcome or value proposition (offer of benefit or value; product/service) that the Value Creator offers to a Value Recipient.

  The Value Proposition, which may be in the form of P.I.G.S., should be designed to relieve the most important pains of the Value Recipient ("pain reliever" approach) and/or create delight ("delight creator" approach).

- **Feedback (F):** Signal, cue, or P.I.G.S. that a Value Recipient or stakeholder provides to a Value Creator. Feedback may be positive as well as negative as a result of experiencing the Output.

In order to quickly describe or sketch how a given organization, business model, or project works, a user must answer a minimum of four Business Model Strip questions as shown below. Subsequent questions can zoom in on the How, for example, how value is created and delivered. This approach allows for both *conceptual and detailed ("zoomable") pain solving*.

o Value Creator (VC) Question: WHO eliminates pain as well as creates, delivers, captures and/or shares value?
o Feedback (F) Question: WHAT is the feedback and/or reward?
o Output (O) Question: WHAT output (product/service) is offered?
o Value Recipient (VR) Question: WHO receives value or benefits?

Business Model Strip with 4 Node-Questions

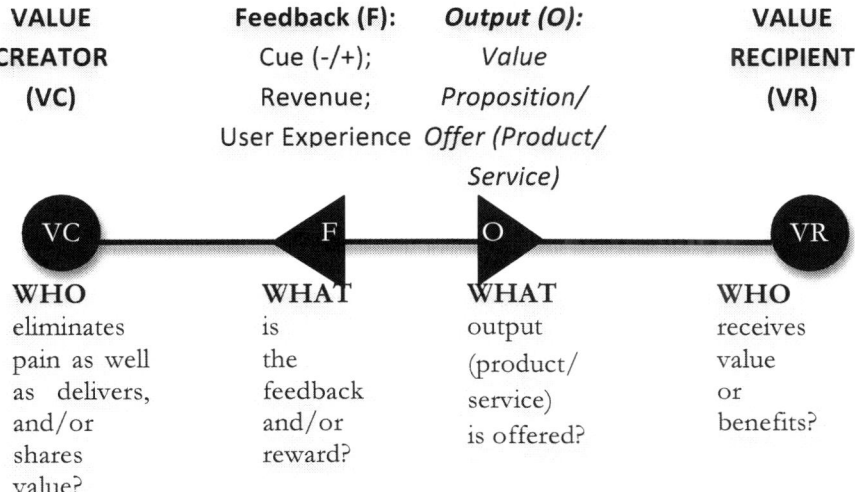

It is important to distinguish between the Business Model Strip of a "pipe" project and that of a "platform" project. A *pipe* Business Model Strip has one customer segment as a Value Recipient (VR). In contrast, a *platform* Business Model Strip consists of two or more integrated Business Model Strips "pipes" that are served by a common set of capability & core values.

Although the classic form of a Business Model Strip is a line diagram with 4 nodes, the diagram *may also be presented in many forms including Fat, Lean, Hybrid, and Punctiform Business Modeling Diagrams.* Below is a presentation of a Business Model Strip in tabular format. Such a "Business Model StripTable" may or may not be used in conjunction with the classic line diagram. Nevertheless, a Business Model StripTable follows the same sequence of description of nodes as in the line diagram. Sticky notes (Post-its) may or may not be used in conjunction with a Business Model Strip.

Business Model StripTable: *4 Value Creator Perspectives (Nodes; Atoms)*

VALUE CREATOR (VC)	Feedback (F): Cue (-/+); Revenue	Value Proposition (VP): Offer (Product/Service)	VALUE RECIPIENT (VR)

One advantage of using a Business Model StripTable is that it could be used for easily and quickly presenting both pipe and platform business models. "Pipe" business models focus on a single customer segment and PSQ, while "platform" business models deal with at least two customer segments or PSQs. A Business Model StripTable can be customized to include a column for "Channels/Customer Relationships" so that it can more fully illustrate how a Value Creator creates and delivers value to a Value Recipient as in a supply chain. But, perhaps the greatest advantage of using a Business Model StripTable is to present a population of business models such as in alternative or "best practice" business models within given sectors and in different industries. Also, a tool such as the Value Proposition Canvas can directly and severally be used within a Business Model StripTable.

A Business Model StripTable for a book publishing project is shown below; the main source of information is the Business Model Generation book. The table is presented in two parts. Part 1 deals with pipe business models for publishing a book while Part 2 deals with platform business models.

Business Model StripTable – Part 1: *Pipe* **Business Models (Projects)**

Project Goal or Job To Get Done (JTGD): Publish a novel book while resolving the pain of [readers]
PSQ: *How Might We Eliminate Pain (HMWEP) of X?*

VALUE CREATOR (VC) - Author *PIPE* ... for ...	Feedback (F): Cue (-/+); UX; Revenue	Value Proposition (VP): Offer (Product/Service)	VALUE RECIPIENT (VR)
Traditionally Published Book Project	Royalties (~10%)	Traditionally Printed Book	Reader *(Channel: Traditional Publisher/Retailer)*
Published-on-Demand Book Project	Royalties (~30%)	Printed-on-demand Book	Reader *(Channel: Print-on-Demand Publisher Lulu.com)*
Do-It-Yourself Book Project	Own Margin; Amazon's Advantage	Self published Book	Reader *(Channel: Own Channel; Amazon)*
Customized Book Project		Book Modules (Chapters)	Reader *(Channel: Own Channel; Amazon)*

Business Model StripTable – Part 2: *Platform* **Business Models (Projects)**

Project Goal or Job To Get Done (JTGD): Publish a novel book while resolving the pain of [readers/users/sponsors]
PSQ: *How Might We Eliminate Pain (HMWEP) of X?*

VALUE CREATOR (VC) - Author *PLATFORM* ... for ...	Feedback (F): Cue (-/+); UX; Revenue	Value Proposition (VP): Offer (Product/Service)	VALUE RECIPIENT (VR)
Free Marketing Book Project	Free (User Data)	Free Book	Reader *(Channel: Personal)*
	Sale of Other Services/Prod.	Author's Related Services/Products	User of Services *(Channel: Personal)*
Co-creation Book Project	Pre-order (Advance Sale)	Co-created Book (Modules)	Co-creating Authors *(Channel: Personal)*
	Point of Sale	Printed Co-created Book	Reader *(Channel: External)*
eBook & Printed Book Project	Subscription Fee	eBook	'Online' Reader *(Channel: Online)*
	Asset Sale	Printed Book	'Offline' Reader *(Channel: Personal)*
Sponsored Book Project	Free (User Data)	Printed Book (With Sponsored Content)	Reader *(Channel: Personal)*
	Sponsoring Fee		Sponsor *(Channel: Personal)*
			Sponsor's Client *(Channel: Sponsor's Channels)*

The Business Model Strip seems to work as a universal tool for rapidly mapping the feedback loop in the business model of pipe and platform projects. **But, where did the Business Model Strip come from? What is its theoretical foundation?**

As mentioned before, the basic model for a transaction, conversation, communication, or exchange between two "living" systems in a project, consists of a Value Creator on the one hand and a Value Recipient on the other hand. The table below shows business and non-business domains to which the 4 nodes of the Business Model Strip can be applied.

Business Model Strip: Elements of Value Creator Chain/Loops for Answering a Pain Solving Question (PSQ)

Subject	Reaction *Verb (Process/Action)*	Object	Stakeholder *Channel*
VALUE CREATOR (VC)	**Feedback (F):** Cue (-/+); UX; Revenue	**Value Proposition (VP):** Offer (Product/Service)	**VALUE RECIPIENT (VR)**
Subject	**Feedback**	**Object**	**Stakeholder**
Supplier/Input/ Processing	**Feedback** (Impact: -/+)	**Output** (Outcome)	**Customer/ Stakeholder**
Supplier (Producer; Seller; Performer)	**P.I.G.S.:** Product; Information; Goods; Service	**P.I.G.S.:** Product; Information; Goods; Service	**Customer** (Consumer; User; Buyer; Demander)
How	Why	What	Who
Infra' Owner	Benefit (Cost)	Offer	Customer
Creator/Architect (Designer)			Co-creator (Collaborator)
Sender			Receiver
Performer			Requester
Service Provider (Giver/Donor)			Guest (Beneficiary)
Actor (Player)			Audience
Care Giver			Patient/Taker
Protagonist			Antagonist
Prosecutor			Defender
Value Destroyer (Persecutor)			Victim (Rescuer)

Structurally, the Business Model Strip can be presented in 2D as a feedback loop or cycle. However, for simplicity, the loop or cycle of a Business Model Strip is usually "collapsed" or flattened into a line or strip. The figures below show two perspectives of a Business Model Strip as a loop or cycle. The first diagram presents the Business Model Strip from a semantic (conversation) perspective while the other diagram shows the Business Model Strip from a business perspective. Each is a circular cause-and-effect diagram.

Business Model StripLoop: Semantic Transaction (Conversation) Model and Perspective *for Answering a Pain Solving Question*

Sense-and-Respond Conversation Loop

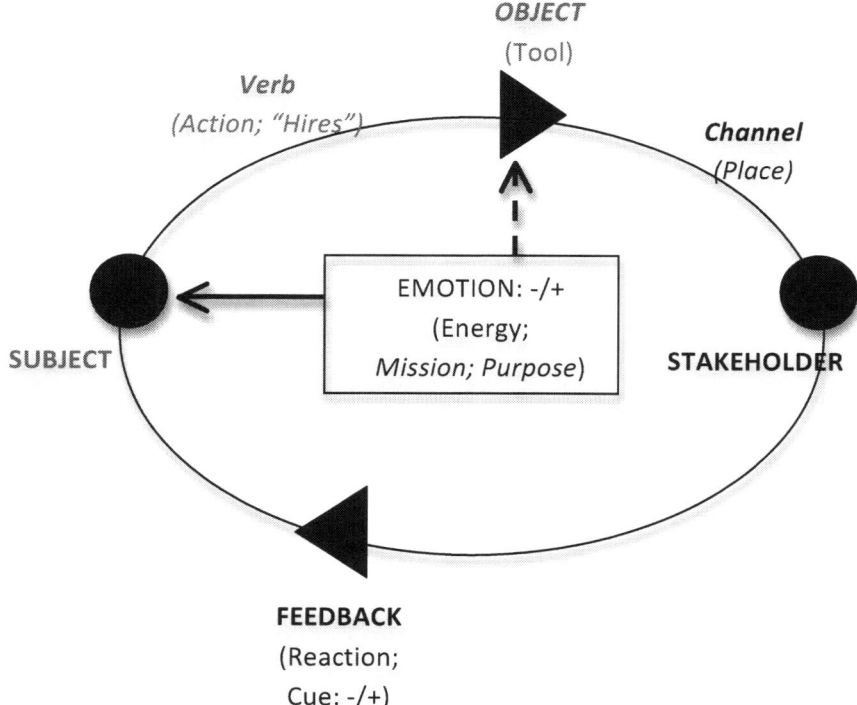

Business Model Strip: 1 Line & 4 Nodes ("Atoms")

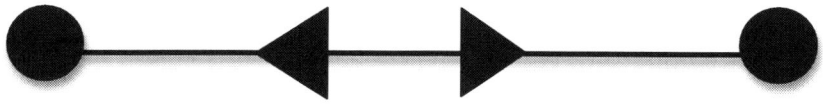

Business Model StripLoop: Business Transaction (Trade; Product Line) Model and Perspective *for Answering a Pain Solving Question*

Sense-and-Respond Trade Loop

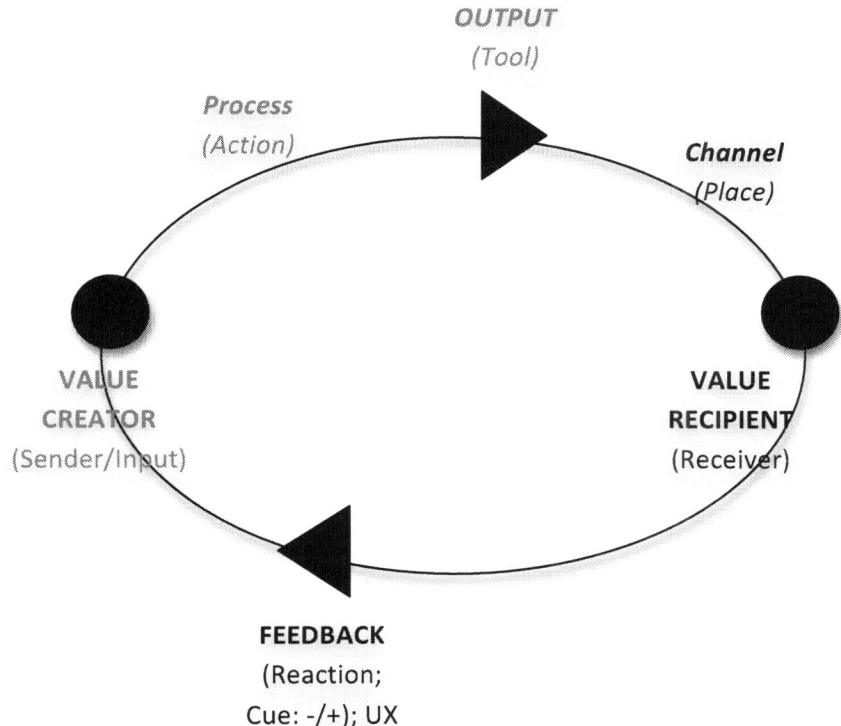

Business Model Strip: One Line Business Model (OLBM)

Many types of business modeling tools and frameworks as well as project planning and management tools can be directly superimposed on a Business Model StripLoop as well as Business Model Strip. The diagram below shows how the *Lean Startup process of the "Build-Measure-Learn (BML)" Loop as well as a marketing funnel ("Pirate Metrics")* may be added to a Business Model StripLoop in order to facilitate conversations on building a startup as well as to improve sale of a given output (tool: value proposition/product).

Business Model StripLoop: Business Transaction and Perspective with Marketing Funnel *for Answering a Pain Solving Question*

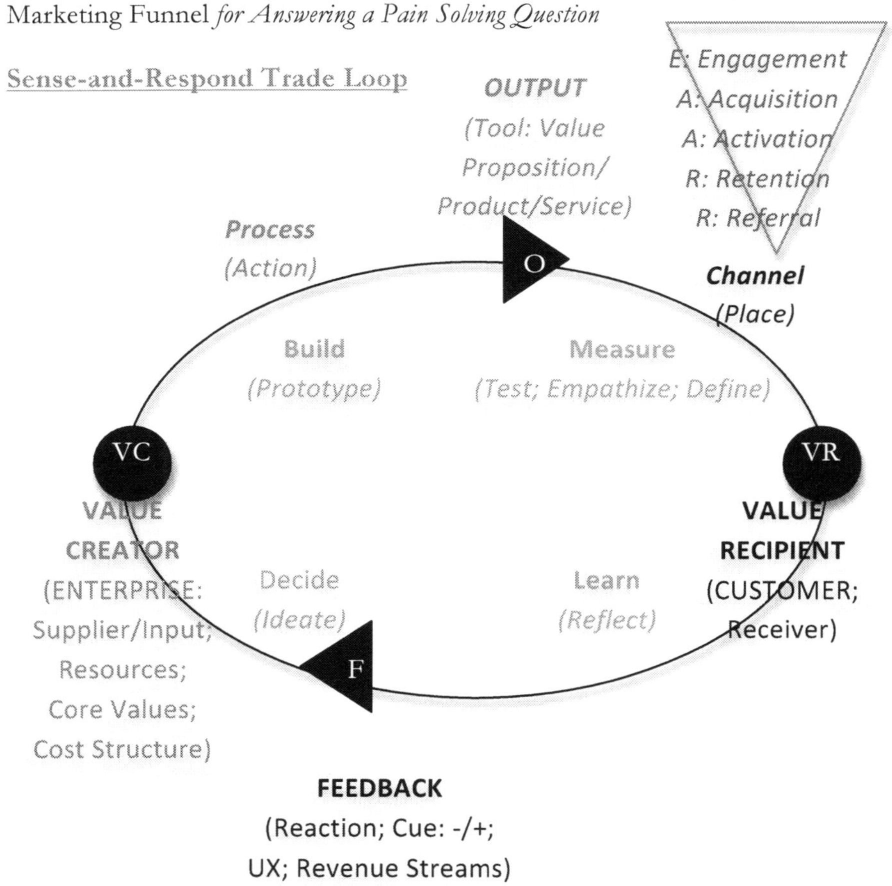

Sense-and-Respond Trade Loop

OUTPUT
(Tool: Value Proposition/ Product/Service)

E: Engagement
A: Acquisition
A: Activation
R: Retention
R: Referral

Process
(Action)

O

Channel
(Place)

Build
(Prototype)

Measure
(Test; Empathize; Define)

VC

VR

VALUE CREATOR
(ENTERPRISE: Supplier/Input; Resources; Core Values; Cost Structure)

Decide
(Ideate)

F

Learn
(Reflect)

VALUE RECIPIENT
(CUSTOMER; Receiver)

FEEDBACK
(Reaction; Cue: -/+;
UX; Revenue Streams)

Business Model Strip: One Line Business Model (OLBM) with Labels

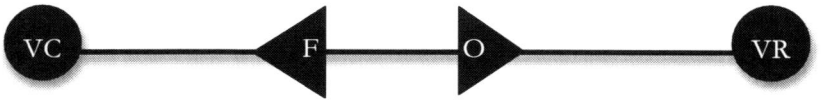

The Sense-and-Respond (Feedback) Loop below shows a superimposition of the Pain-Plan-Do-Review (PPDR) Cycle) on the Business Model Strip Loop. Since the PPDR Cycle is a tool for Universal Pain Solving & Project Management, the steps of any pain solving tool, process, or procedure such as in Total Design Thinking ("EDIPTR"), Six Sigma ("DMAIC"), and Kanban Board can be mapped on nodes of a Business Model StripLoop.

Business Model StripLoop: Business Transaction and Perspective in Conjunction with Pain-Plan-Do-Review (PPDR) Cycle

Sense-and-Respond Trade Loop

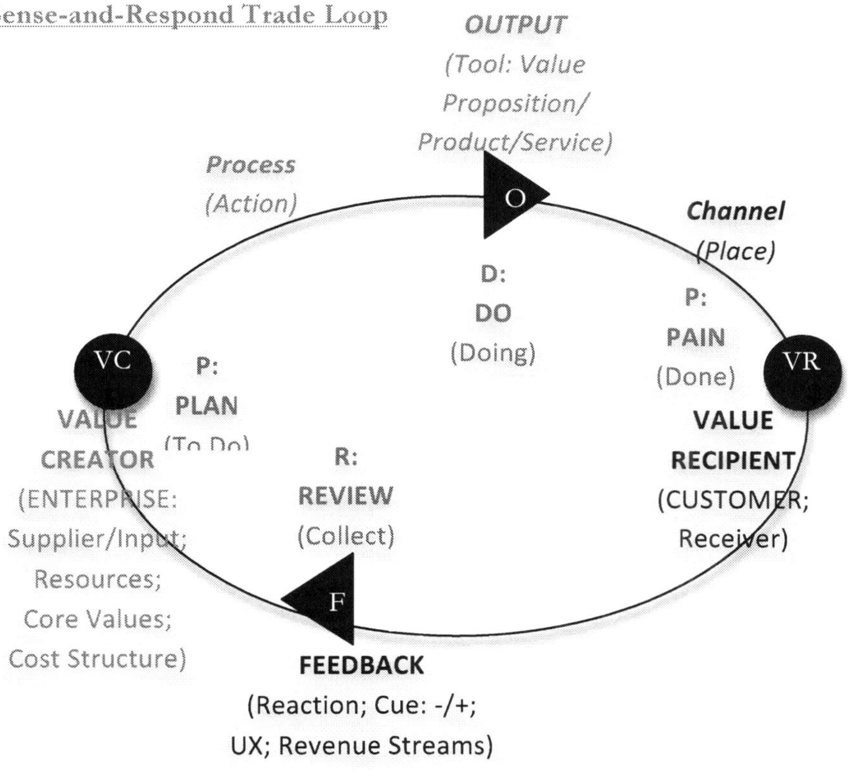

OUTPUT
(Tool: Value
Proposition/
Product/Service)

Process
(Action)

O

Channel
(Place)

D:
DO
(Doing)

P:
PAIN
(Done)

VC

P:
PLAN
(To Do)

VR

VALUE
CREATOR
(ENTERPRISE:
Supplier/Input;
Resources;
Core Values;
Cost Structure)

R:
REVIEW
(Collect)

VALUE
RECIPIENT
(CUSTOMER;
Receiver)

F

FEEDBACK
(Reaction; Cue: -/+;
UX; Revenue Streams)

Business Model Strip: One Line Business Model (OLBM)

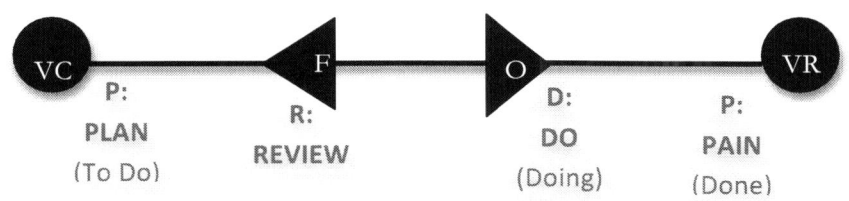

VC

P:
PLAN
(To Do)

F

R:
REVIEW

O

D:
DO
(Doing)

P:
PAIN
(Done)

VR

In terms of modular worksheets for use in conjunction with a Business Model Strip, each node may be regarded as a trade-off map. Consequently, four trade-off maps of a Business Model Strip are as follows: Value Creator (VC) Trade-off Map; Feedback (F) Trade-off Map; Output (O) Trade-off Map; Value Recipient (VR) Trade-off Map. Each Trade-off Map is defined by at least four categories of properties: Name; Purpose/Functionality/Job To Get Done; Delight Pain. For a given Purpose/Functionality/Job To Get Done, the survival and prosperity of each node depends on maximization of delight and minimization of pain.

The four trade-off nodes of a Business Model Strip can be grouped or categorized in several ways. To facilitate discussions regarding rapid and successful development of organizations especially startups, the nodes can be put into two categories: "FrontStage nodes" and "BackStage nodes." The nodes of Output (Product/Service) and Value Recipient (Customer) constitute the FrontStage nodes, which are especially important to startups that are focusing on achieving Problem-Solution Fit as well as Product-Market Fit. FrontStage nodes are also the focus of companies such as Apple and Amazon, their competitive advantage of which largely depends on the disciplines of "Product Leadership" and "Customer Intimacy."

In contrast to the FrontStage nodes, which are customer-facing and rely on "Customer Intimacy" activities to deliver the Value Proposition, the BackStage nodes are enterprise-facing and depend on the discipline of "Operational Excellence" to create and offer the Value Proposition. The two nodes of the BackStage are Value Creator (Enterpise) and Feedback (Cue; Impacts). The diagram below shows the front and backstages nodes of the 'theater' that is a Business Model Strip.

Business Model Strip Illustrating Front and BackStage Nodes

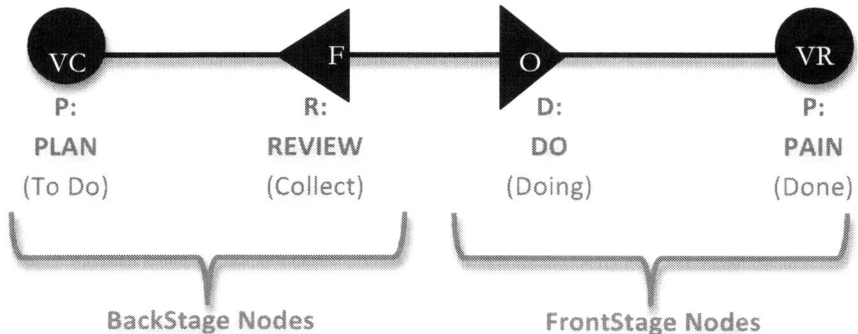

Finally, the basic content, structure, and logic of a Business Model Strip can be alternatively and visually expressed using a meso-canvas as shown below. The template of the Business Model StripLoop Meso-Canvas facilitates integration of the Sense-and-Respond (Feedback) Loop with the framework of the classic Business Model Canvas especially in continuous pain solving projects.

Business Model StripLoop Meso-Canvas: Sense and Respond Loop **with** 4 Categories of Topics for Value Creator Perspectives

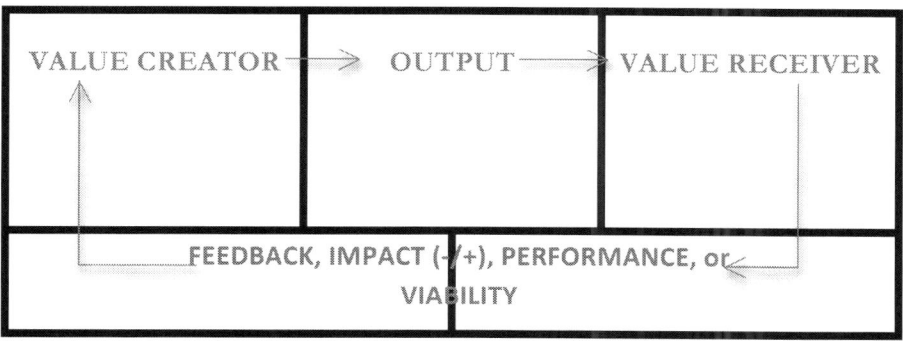

Business Model StripLoop Meso-Canavas: Sense and Respond Loop with Question-tags and Topics of Kanban Board

VALUE CREATOR *(HOW)*	OUTPUT *(WHAT)*	VALUE RECEIVER *(WHO)*
P: PLAN (To Do) -----------	**D: DO** (Doing) -----------	**P: PAIN** (Done) -----------
FEEDBACK, IMPACT (-/+), PERFORMANCE, or VIABILITY *(WHY)*		
R: REVIEW		(Collect)

Business Model StripLoop Meso-Canavas: Sense and Respond Loop with Question-tags and Topics of Kanban Board as well as POKER Cycle

VALUE CREATOR (HOW)	OUTPUT (WHAT)	VALUE RECEIVER (WHO)
P: PLAN (To Do)	D: DO (Doing)	P: PAIN (Done)
-------------	-------------	-------------
Experiments	Objectives	Pain
	Key Results	
FEEDBACK, IMPACT (-/+), PERFORMANCE, or VIABILITY (WHY)		
R: REVIEW	Review	(Collect)

Note
POKER is an acronym for Pain; Objectives; Key Objectives; Experiments; Review.
As can be seen above, POKER is directly related to the four nodes of the Business Model Strip and Question-tags as well as the cycle of Pain-Plan-Do-Review (PPDR) and Kanban board. In fact, POKER is a slight elaboration of the PPDR where "Plan" is replaced by two topics: "Objectives" and "Key Results."

Also, the Business Model StripLoop Meso-Canvas can be replaced by the more user-friendly term of **"POKER Canvas."** It is important to note that the acronym of "POKER" indicates the order in which the meso-blocks are recommended to be completed.

Although the focus in this book is on the PPDR Cycle, it should be noted that the PPDR Cycle and the POKER Cycle are synonymous or equivalent.

8 FRACTAL DIAMOND MODELING (FDM) LANGUAGE: A SHORTHAND FOR *MULTILEVEL PROTOTYPING* OF PIPE & PLATFORM PROJECTS

In the world today, there are **billions of pains-to-be-solved and projects ("jobs to get done")** in both for-profit and non-profit sectors of the global economy. Each project or pain-to-be-solved requires a viable and transparent business model so that stakeholders can not only more clearly see how different resources come together but also manage these resources in order to effectively and efficiently achieve the project's vision, goal, or job to get done. However, the failure rate of business models in innovation projects is alarming. The failure rate of innovation projects and consequently, their business models is estimated at a minimum of 90%; more conservative estimates put the failure rate of innovation projects at 70%. In any case, the failure rate of innovation projects is high and unacceptable. Such failures represent a huge waste of resources especially in terms of money, energy, and time for resolving pains in organizations.

In the world of business startups, the failure rate of 90% seems more plausible than that of 70%. Thought leaders such as Steve Blank have 'held accountable' use of the traditional and voluminous business plan which is ill-adapted for resolving pain in volatile, uncertain, complex, and ambiguous environment such as in an innovation startup. In a traditional business plan, a business model is textual rather than visual. In recent years, therefore, Steve Blank and the Lean Startup Movement have welcomed the Business Model Canvas as a visual, flexible, and useful tool for rapidly prototyping and presenting business models in the past, present, and future. At least, the Business Model Canvas is reducing the cost of failure as well as waste of resources especially by innovation startups that would have otherwise had to deploy written inordinately long and rigid business plans.

Business and Non-Profit Organizations around the world are adopting the Business Model Canvas as the *de facto* tool for visually documenting business models as well as resolving pain of stakeholders. At the moment, the Business Model Canvas provides a common register of 9 topics and visual language (9 tessellated building blocs of a canvas) for prototyping as well as presenting business models. *But does the Business Model Canvas provide the best tool and language for rapidly resolving pain as well as prototyping pipe and platform projects at the 4E-levels: Enterprise; Ecosystem; Economy; Environment?* The diagram below shows a Shared Value Map that illustrates the level of each of the 4Es: Enterprise; Ecosystem; Economy; Environment.

Shared Value Map: Multilevel Spatial Hierarchy of Enterprise, Ecosystem, Economy, and Environment (4E) *for Resolving Pain at a Given Point in Time*

Pain Solving Question (PSQ): ....

WHERE:

The 4E-levels of the above Shared Value Map contrasts that of the two levels of the Business Model Environment (BME) diagram in the Business Model Generation book. Osterwalder et al do not hierarchically distinguish levels in the Business Model Environment. Instead, they consider the BME as a unitary space of 4 forces: Industry & Market *(cf. Ecosystem);* Macro-economic *(cf. Economy);* Key Trends *(cf. Environment);* compare below.

Shared Value Map: Multilevel Spatial Hierarchy of Enterprise, Ecosystem, Economy, and Environment (4E): *(Players in Economy or Value Net are Shown)*
Pain Solving Question (PSQ): ....
WHERE:

With the multilevel spatial hierarchy of a Shared Value Map, one can repeatedly use the "fractal diamond shape" to answer a Pain Solving Question while systematically analyzing the viability or attractiveness of a business model at the level of the 4E's: Enterprise; Ecosystem; Economy; Environment. Below, a Business Model Strip, which still presents a sense-and-respond (feedback) or conversation loop, is shown in diamond format. In short, a *multilevel sense-and-respond logic is used.*

Business Model Strip in "Diamond" Format for Resolving Pain

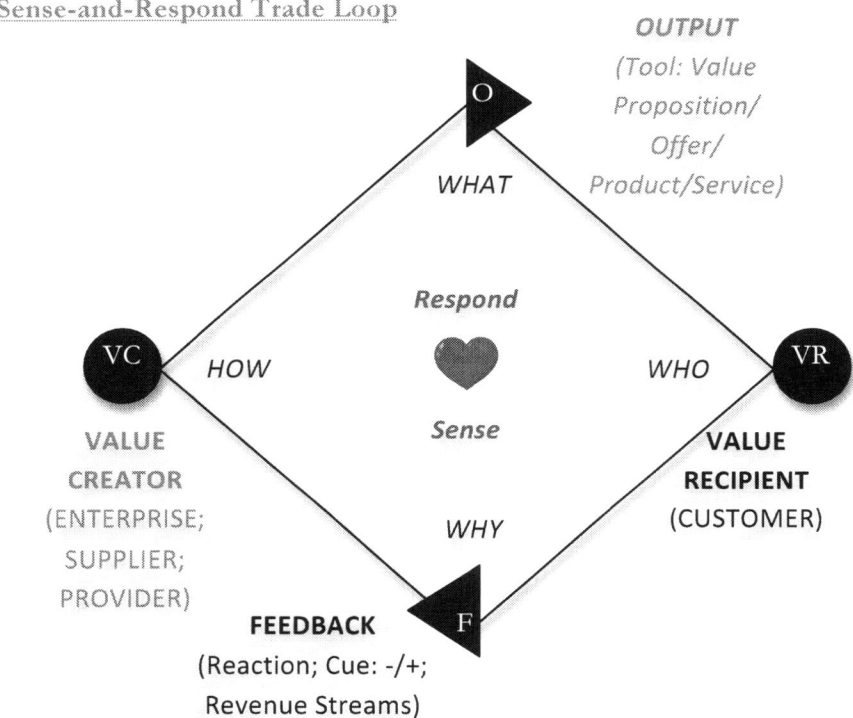

Sense-and-Respond Trade Loop

Business Model Strip: 1 Line & 4 Nodes or "Atoms" (Showing Topics of Pain-Plan-Do-Review (PPDR) Cycle as well as Kanban Board)

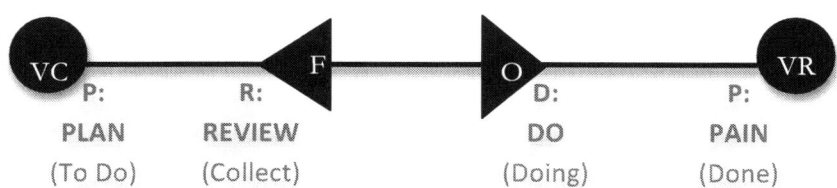

The multilevel sense-and-respond approach contrasts that of the four forces of Osterwalder et al Business Model Environment. In the Business Model Generation book, the four forces of the Business Model Environment have a checklist of tasks and questions to facilitate analysis of the Business Model Environment. Unlike in the multilevel diamond environment of a Shared Value Map, well known tools such as in the Five Forces of Competition and Value Net cannot be directly applied to the Business Model Environment of a Business Model Canvas; there is not a one-to-one correspondence in the visual structural logic of the tools.

Although the Business Model Canvas presents several examples of platforms that have two or three-sided markets, the Canvas is optimized for presenting a pipe business model with a single market or one-sided customer segment. When platforms are featured on a Business Model Canvas, color coding and/or arrows indicating flow of resources are often used. Diagrams of the Business Model Canvas for platforms look unwieldy and confusing as well as difficult to interpret. At best, each customer segment should have its own Business Model Strip or Business Model Canvas so that lines of business models can be clearly observed in terms of their complementarities and conflicts.

Through my research on the evolution of systems, I've observed that **"living" objects or systems generally cyclically evolve using four organizational structures: Stone-heap (Point); Chain (Line/Pipe); Tree (V-shape/Hierarchy/Platform); Network (Web/Diamond/Platform).** Business Models are no exception to this trend in the evolution of organizational structures. Consequently, business model pipes are frequently being disrupted by business model platforms in today's (global) economy. This trend puts a limit on the use of the Business Model Canvas for rapidly prototyping platforms since using a Business Model Canvas requires far more resources than in using a Business Model Strip.

For a provider with a three-sided market, the ultimate platform is in the shape of a tetrahedron or diamond where all edges are linked. A nested diamond shape or "C.O.P.S. Diamond" can be used to show the 4E-levels of a business model. The acronym, C.O.P..S. stands for Customers; Other Parties; Provider; Suppliers. At the enterprise level, the framework of a C.O.P.S. Diamond can be used to show a 1, 2, or 3-sided business model. The following set of diagrams first shows the template of a Shared Value Map with a C.O.P.S. Diamond. Then follow Shared Value Maps for one, two, and three-sided markets. It is important to note that for an organization with 4 or more markets, an n-sided polygon replaces the diamond shape; n is a number starting from 5.

Shared Value Map: Multilevel Spatial Hierarchy of Enterprise, Ecosystem, Economy, and Environment (4E) *for Pipe and Platform Business Models/Projects*

WHEN: Future *(To Do)*/Present *(Doing)*/Past *(Done)*
Stakeholder: ....
Project Goal or Job To Get Done (JTGD): ....
Value: Benefit/Cost or **Delight/Pain (+/-)**........................
Pain Solving Question (PSQ): ....
WHERE:

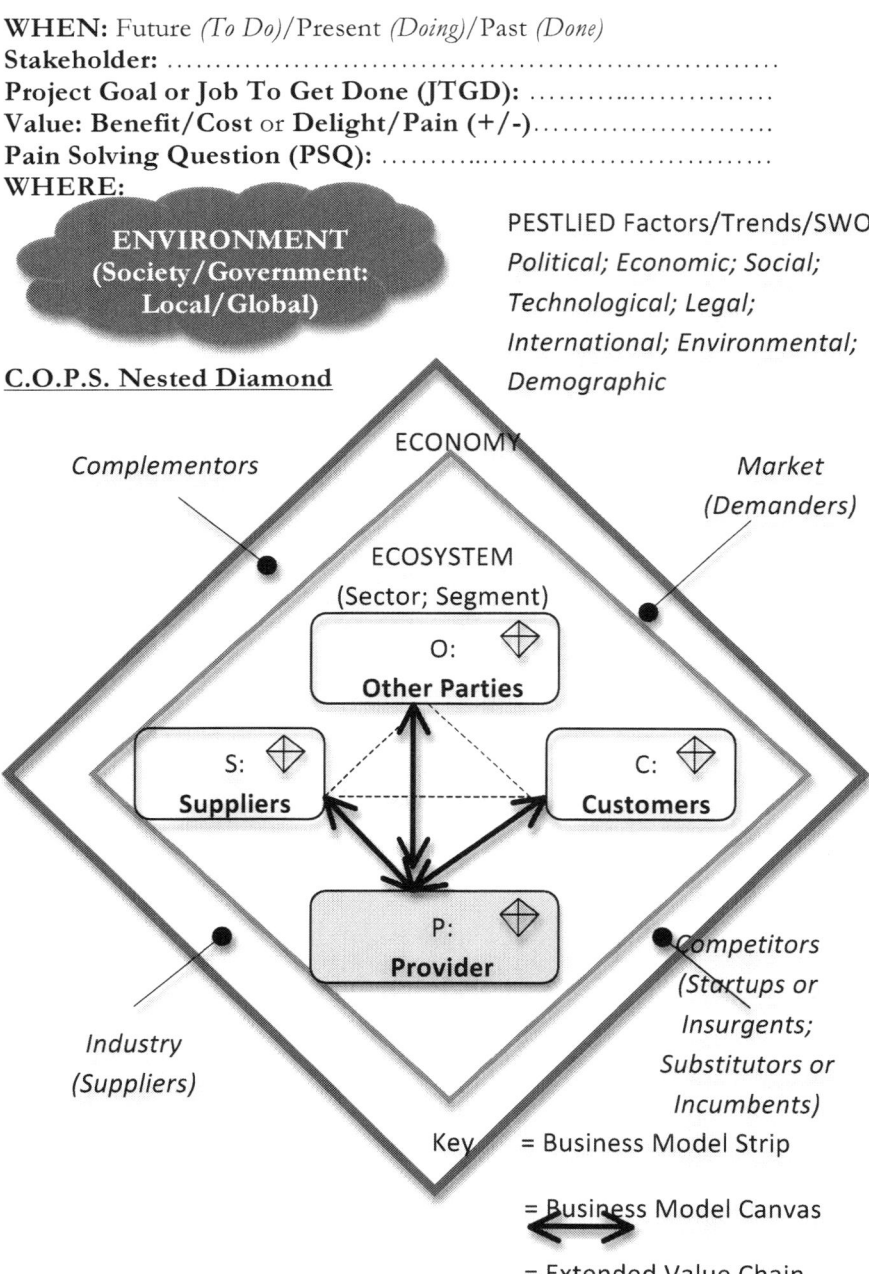

PESTLIED Factors/Trends/SWOT:
Political; Economic; Social;
Technological; Legal;
International; Environmental;
Demographic

Key: = Business Model Strip

= Business Model Canvas

= Extended Value Chain

74

Shared Value Map for <u>Pipe Project</u> to Answer Pain Solving Question

WHEN: Future *(To Do)*/Present *(Doing)*/Past *(Done)*
Stakeholder: ....
Project Goal or Job To Get Done (JTGD): ....
Value: Benefit/Cost or **Delight/Pain (+/-)**.......................
Pain Solving Question (PSQ): ....
WHERE:

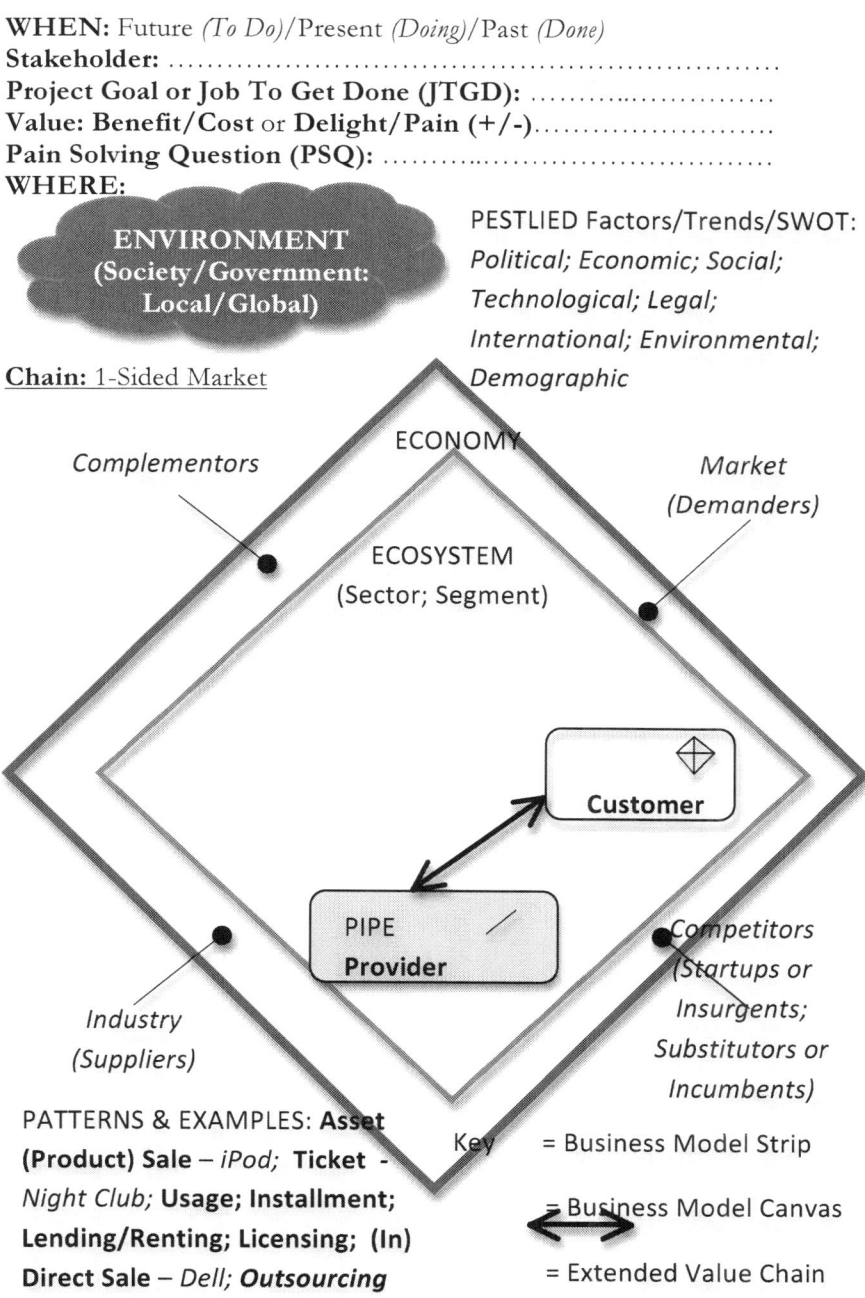

ENVIRONMENT
(Society/Government:
Local/Global)

PESTLIED Factors/Trends/SWOT:
Political; Economic; Social;
Technological; Legal;
International; Environmental;
Demographic

Chain: <u>1-Sided Market</u>

ECONOMY

Complementors

Market
(Demanders)

ECOSYSTEM
(Sector; Segment)

Customer

PIPE
Provider

Competitors
(Startups or
Insurgents;
Substitutors or
Incumbents)

Industry
(Suppliers)

PATTERNS & EXAMPLES: **Asset**
(Product) Sale – *iPod;* **Ticket -**
Night Club; **Usage; Installment;**
Lending/Renting; Licensing; (In)
Direct Sale – *Dell;* **Outsourcing**

Key   = Business Model Strip

= Business Model Canvas

= Extended Value Chain

Shared Value Map for <u>2-Sided Platform Project</u> to Answer Pain Solving Question

WHEN: Future *(To Do)*/Present *(Doing)*/Past *(Done)*
Stakeholder: ....
Project Goal or Job To Get Done (JTGD): ....…..............
Value: Benefit/Cost or **Delight/Pain (+/-)**........................
Pain Solving Question (PSQ): ....…..............................
WHERE: PESTLIED

ENVIRONMENT
(Society/Government:
Local/Global)

Factors/Trends/SWOT:
Political; Economic; Social;
Technological; Legal;
International; Environmental;

<u>Valley</u> (Un/Coupled): 2-Sided Market *Demographic*

ECONOMY

Complementors

Market
(Demanders)

ECOSYSTEM
(Sector; Segment)

Customer 2

Customer 1

PLATFORM
Provider

Competitors
(Startups or
Insurgents;
Substitutors or
Incumbents)

Industry
(Suppliers)

PATTERNS & EXAMPLES: **Freemium** -
Radio; TV +/- Ads; Skype; **Franchising***;*
Bait & Hook *– Gillette;* **Brokerage** –
Bank; Real Estate; **Co-develop** *– P &G;*
Matchmaker: *Dating Club;* **Mall/Park**

Key   = Business Model Strip

= Business Model Canvas

= Extended Value Chain

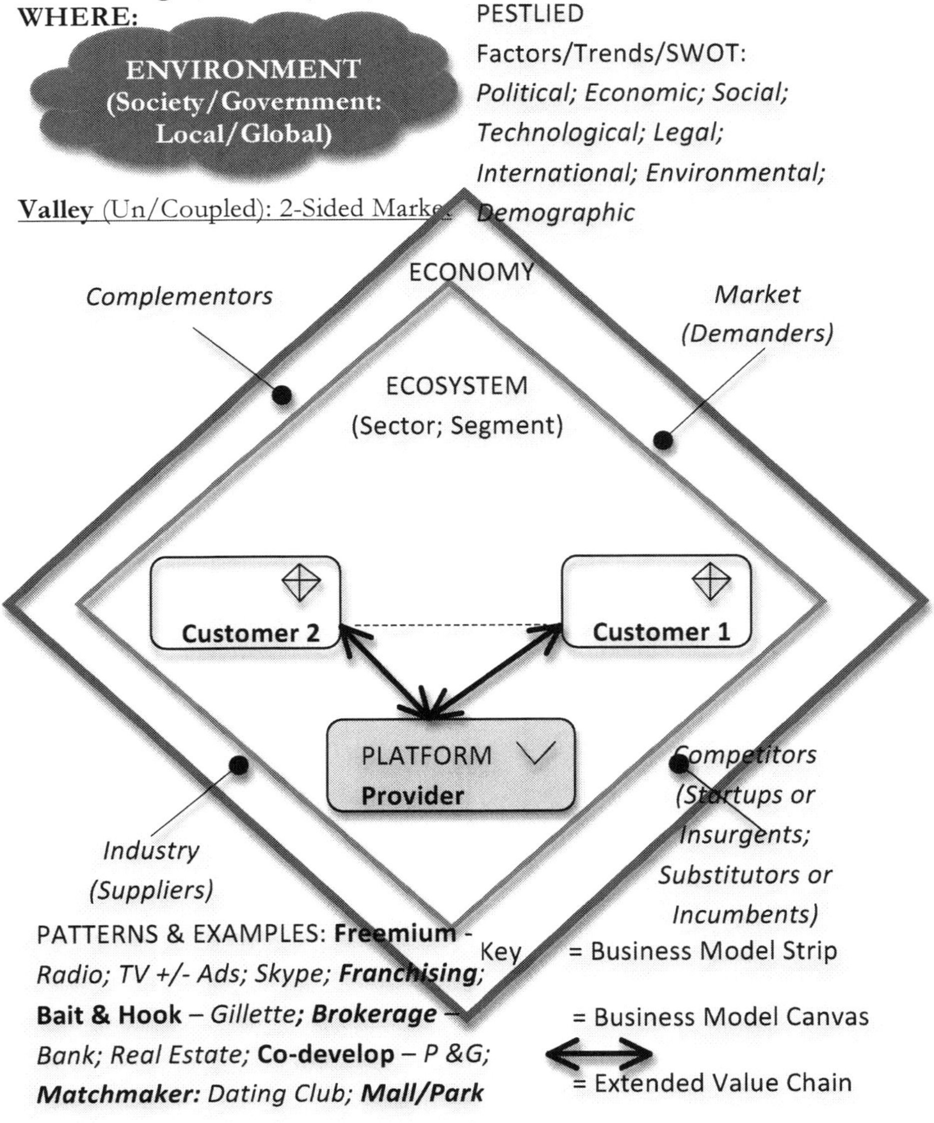

Shared Value Map for <u>3-Sided Platform Project</u> to Answer Pain Solving Question
WHEN: Future *(To Do)*/Present *(Doing)*/Past *(Done)*
Stakeholder: ....
Project Goal or Job To Get Done (JTGD): ....
Value: Benefit/Cost or **Delight/Pain (+/-)** ....
Pain Solving Question (PSQ): ....
WHERE:

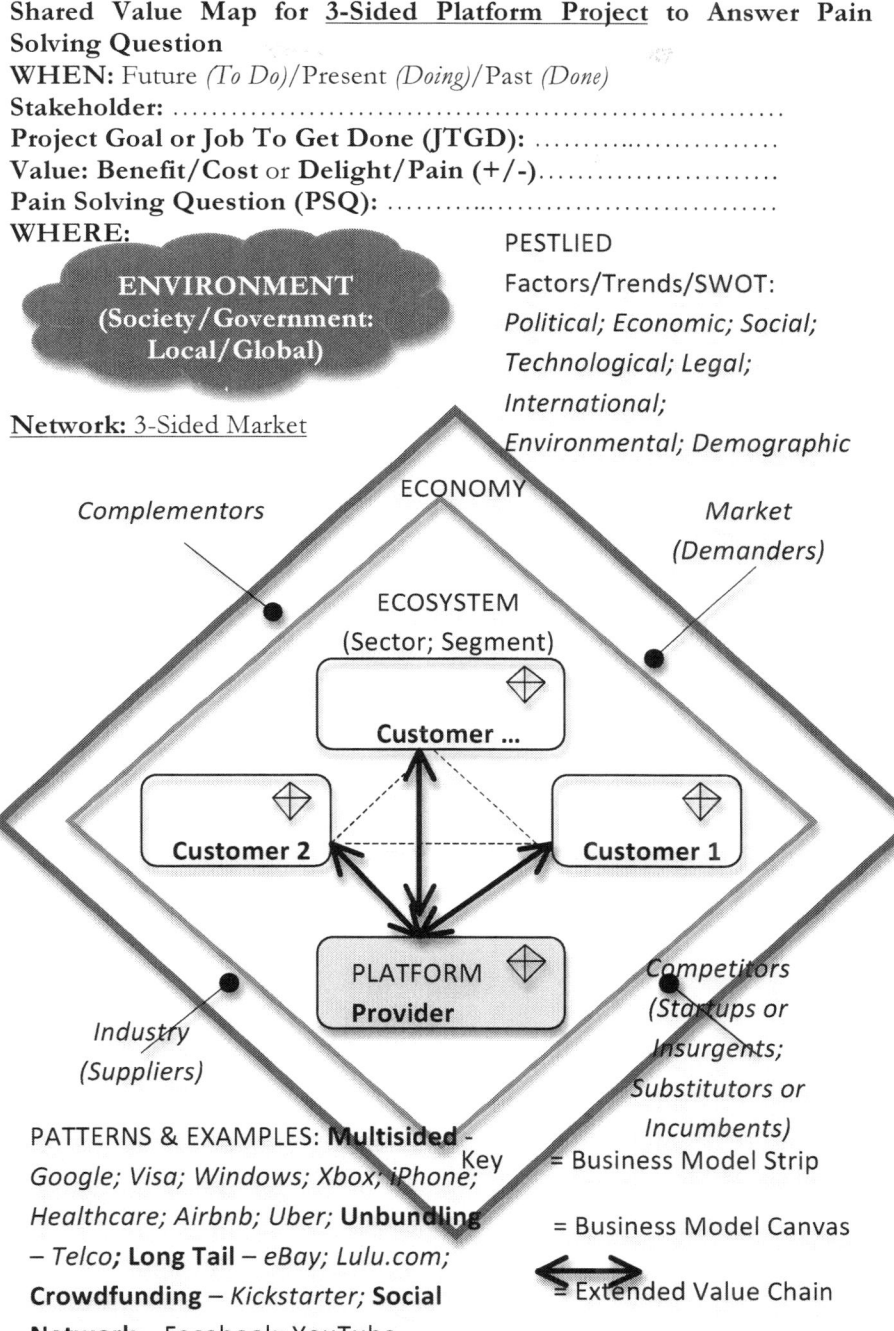

PESTLIED
Factors/Trends/SWOT:
Political; Economic; Social;
Technological; Legal;
International;
Environmental; Demographic

ENVIRONMENT
(Society/Government:
Local/Global)

Network: 3-Sided Market

ECONOMY

Complementors

Market (Demanders)

ECOSYSTEM
(Sector; Segment)

Customer ...

Customer 2   **Customer 1**

PLATFORM
Provider

Competitors (Startups or Insurgents; Substitutors or Incumbents)

Industry (Suppliers)

PATTERNS & EXAMPLES: **Multisided** – *Google; Visa; Windows; Xbox; iPhone; Healthcare; Airbnb; Uber;* **Unbundling** – *Telco;* **Long Tail** – *eBay; Lulu.com;* **Crowdfunding** – *Kickstarter;* **Social Network** – Facebook; YouTube

Key = Business Model Strip

= Business Model Canvas

= Extended Value Chain

To highlight the similarities and differences between the multilevel approach of the Shared Value Map and two level approach of the Business Model Environment for answering a Pain Solving Question (PSQ), a Shared Value Map for the Pharmaceutical Industry (in the USA) is presented. A similar example of the Business Model Environment for the Pharmaceutical Industry is given in the Business Model Generation book.

The Shared Value Map indicates that, at the level of the ecosystem, the Pharmaceutical Industry is organized as a platform of providers (pharmaceutical and biotechnology manufacturers) offering products to a pharmaceutical market of hospitals, pharmacies, and physicians. Delivery takes place through several channels: wholesale; mail orders; group purchasing organizations. Complementors include medical device manufacturers and IT firms that focus on improving healthcare. At the level of the pharmaceutical industry, one could also apply classic tools such as in Porter's Five Forces of Competition Analysis as well as Brandenburger and Nalebuff's Value Net.

At the level of the manufacturing economy, stakeholders include insurers, government agencies, and employees. At the level of the environment, PESTLIED factors and trends as well as SWOT Analysis should be considered. PESTLIED is an acronym for Political; Economic; Social; Technological; Legal; International; Environmental; Demographic. Usually PESTLIED Factors and trends are usually outside the scope of enterprise and should therefore be assumed to be constraints.

At the enterprise level, the Business Model Strip of individual organizations should be explored and documented with a view to adapting to constraints or reconstructing boundaries of the ecosystem, economy, and/or environment. At the enterprise level, any type of analysis or viability study can be done: financial, social, and/or environmental benefit-cost (value) analysis.

Following the Shared Value Map is a Value Engine Map for the Pharmaceutical Industry. The Value Engine Map assumes that the most important pain is "Cost" while the most important delight is "Quality." Generic Strategies are plotted in some cells. With its high quality and high cost, the USA healthcare system is considered to be pursuing a Luxury Spot Strategy and Business Model. Consequently, the mass of the population is underserved. In such a situation, an opportunity exists for the USA's Luxury Spot strategy/business model to be disrupted by a healthcare service that has low cost and 'good enough' quality.

EXAMPLE OF SHARED VALUE MAP: "Sense and Respond"-Pain Solving *for Business Model Pipes & Platforms in Pharmaceutical Ind.*

WHEN: Future *(To Do)*/Present *(Doing)*/Past *(Done)*
Stakeholder: ....
Project Goal or Job To Get Done (JTGD): Instantly Improve Healthcare
Value: Benefit/Cost or **Delight/Pain (+/-)**........................
Pain Solving Question (PSQ): How Might We Eliminate Pain (HMWEP)
of "X": *Customers; Other Parties; Suppliers in Pharmaceutical Ecosystem?*
WHERE: USA

ENVIRONMENT
(Society/Government:
Local/Global)

PESTLIED Factors/Trends/SWOT:
*Political; Economic; Social;
Technological; Legal;
International; Environmental;
Demographic*

Pharmaceutical **C.O.P.S. Diamond**

ECONOMY

Pharmaceutical Complementors

Pharmaceutical Market

ECOSYSTEM
(Sector; Segment)

O:
Other Parties

S:
Suppliers

C:
Customers

P: Pharmaceutical **Provider**

Pharmaceutical Competitors (Startups or Insurgents; Substitutors or Incumbents)

Pharmaceutical Industry (Suppliers)

Key   = Business Model Strip

= Business Model Canvas

= Extended Value Chain

Pain Solving in the Healthcare Industry: Quality vs. Cost Trade-off

Value Engine Map: Business Model Pipes/Platforms for Pharmaceutical Industry (Providers)

>   **Time:** *Past (Done)/Present (Doing)/Future (To Do)*

>   **Goal or Job To Get Done:** Instantly Improve Value of Healthcare

>   **Environment (Context; Location):** …………………...…………....

Ideal Value Proposition (IVP): *Highest Quality of Healthcare at Zero Cost*

	Low (1-3)	Moderate (3-6)	High (6-10)
High (6-10)	**Blue Ocean Value Prop./ Strategy/ Business Model**	Sweet Spot Value Prop./ Strategy/ Business Model	Luxury Spot *(Differentiation)* Value Prop./ Strategy/ Business Model: **USA**
DELIGHT (+): Quality; Performance **Moderate (3-6)**	Disruptive Innovation *(Low Cost)* Value Prop./ Strategy/ Business Model	*Stuck-in-the-Middle* Value Prop./ Strategy/ Business Model	Volcano Value Prop./ Strategy/ Business Model
Low (1-3)	Green Ocean Value Prop./ Strategy/ Business Model	No-Man's-Island Value Prop./ Strategy/ Business Model	Red Ocean Value Prop./ Strategy/ Business Model

Low (1-3)   *Moderate* (3-6)   *High* (6-10)

PAIN (-): Cost

Users of the Business Model Canvas struggle with documenting and designing the business model of Non-Profit Organizations (NPO) while solving the pain of stakeholders. A Mission Model Canvas, which changes the names of some topics, has subsequently been developed. Unlike in the Business Model Canvas, the Mission Model Canvas explicitly includes a box for "Mission (or problem) description." Nevertheless, the Mission Model Canvas is not expressly designed for carrying out social or environmental cost-benefit analysis. Its implicit measure of progress is cost effectiveness.

Perhaps, the greatest weakness of the Mission Model Canvas is its *failure to explicitly note and consider non-profit organizations as platforms*. A non-profit organization is not a pipe. Every non-profit organization relies on donors or grants for its survival, since by definition non-profit organizations do not generate revenue. By not knowing that a non-profit organization is a platform, some users of the Mission Model Canvas may erroneously model non-profit organizations as pipes. With the following line (diamond) diagram of a Shared Value Map for non-profit organizations, it is unlikely that such a mistake will be made. In the Shared Vale Map for Non-Profit Organizations, stakeholders such as beneficiaries, donors/ sponsors, and partners (suppliers) are simply and clearly identified.

In recent years and in the wake of severe climate change such as global warming, the topic of sustainability has come to the fore in the design of business models. Many large corporations are focusing not only on financial profitability but also on social and environmental sustainability. This sustainability approach has much in common with the "triple bottom line" approach that focuses on the 3P's: Profit; People; Planet. Due to the focus of the Business Model Canvas on financial profitability with its description of impacts as "Cost Structure" and "Revenue Streams," the Canvas cannot be directly used for social impact assessment as well as environmental impact assessment. The Canvas's two impact topics have to be modified.

Business Model Practitioners dealing with social and/or sustainable enterprises have responded in two main ways regarding their use of the Business Model Canvas. Some Social entrepreneurs have added blocks for topics such as Mission while others have modified existing topics of the Business Model Canvas; an example of the latter is in changing "Customers" to "Beneficiaries." Since the approach of the Shared Value Map focuses on symbolic rather than textual descriptions of its nodes and links on a Business Model Strip, domain specific descriptions can always be added. Consequently, the Business Model Strip facilitates "Tri-Benefit-Cost-Analysis." Financial, Social, and Environmental Benefit-Cost Analysis can independently be done for a given sustainability Shared Value Map.

SHARED VALUE MAP for Non-Profit Organizations (NPO): **"Sense and Respond"-Pain Solving** *for Business Model Pipes & Platforms in Non-profit Sector*
WHEN: Future *(To Do)*/Present *(Doing)*/Past *(Done)*
Stakeholder: ....
Project Goal or Job To Get Done (JTGD): ....
Value: Benefit/Cost or **Delight/Pain (+/-)** ....
Pain Solving Question (PSQ): How Might We Eliminate Pain (HMWEP) of "X": *Beneficiary; Donors/Sponsors; Partners (Suppliers)*?
WHERE:

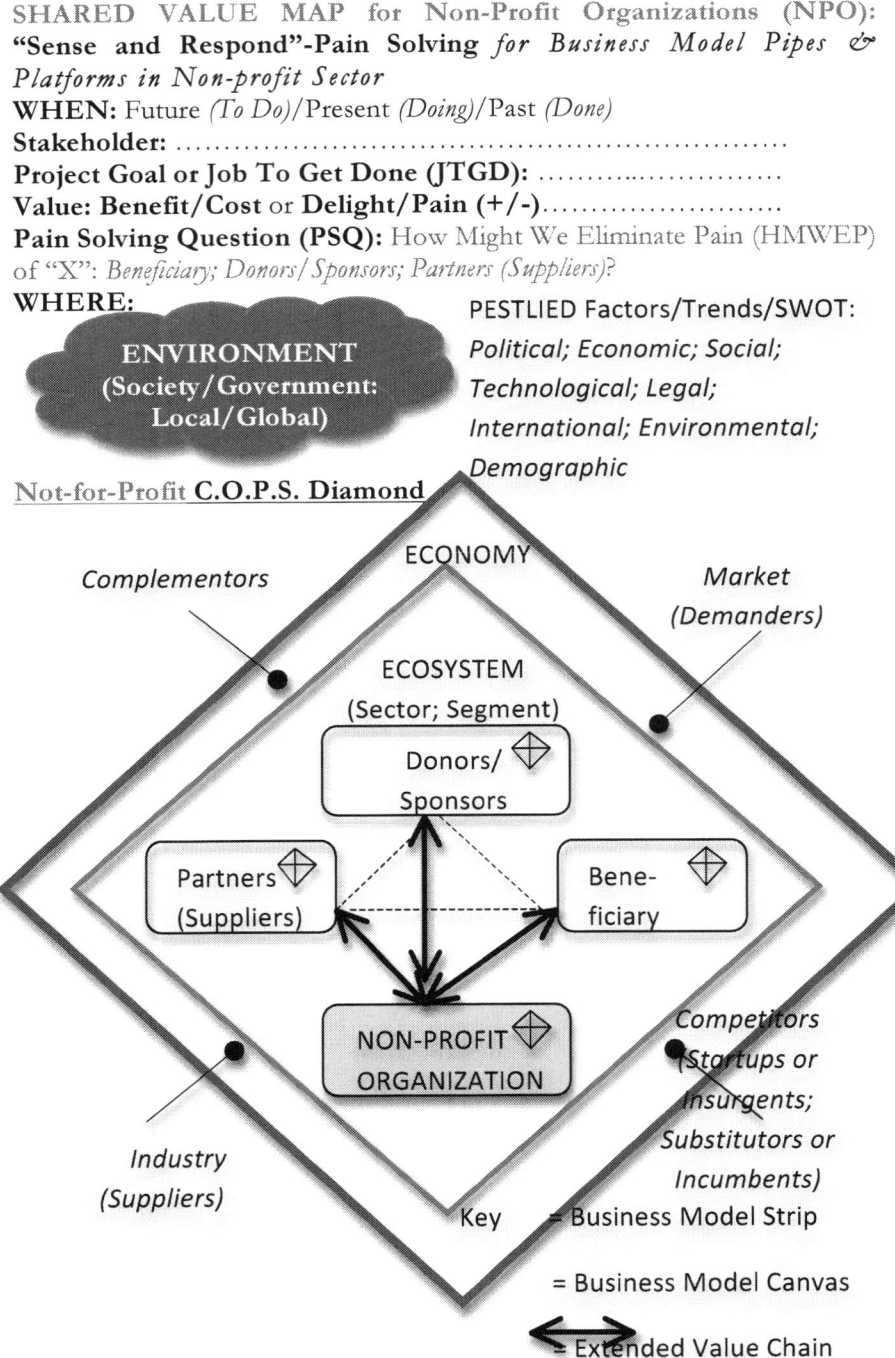

PESTLIED Factors/Trends/SWOT:
Political; Economic; Social;
Technological; Legal;
International; Environmental;
Demographic

ENVIRONMENT
(Society/Government:
Local/Global)

Not-for-Profit **C.O.P.S. Diamond**

ECONOMY

Complementors

Market (Demanders)

ECOSYSTEM
(Sector; Segment)

Donors/Sponsors

Partners (Suppliers)

Bene-ficiary

NON-PROFIT ORGANIZATION

Competitors
(Startups or Insurgents; Substitutors or Incumbents)

Industry (Suppliers)

Key = Business Model Strip

= Business Model Canvas

= Extended Value Chain

SHARED VALUE MAP for Profitable Sustainable Organizations (PSO): **"Sense and Respond"-Pain Solving** *for Business Model Pipes & Platforms in Sustainability Sector*

WHEN: Future *(To Do)*/Present *(Doing)*/Past *(Done)*

Stakeholder: ....

Project Goal or Job To Get Done (JTGD): ....

Pain Solving Question (PSQ): How Might We Eliminate Pain (HMWEP) of "X": *Co-creator (Customer); Governors (Other Parties); Partners (Suppliers)?*

WHERE:

PESTLIED Factors/Trends/SWOT:

ENVIRONMENT (Society/Government: Local/Global)

Political; Economic; Social; Technological; Legal; International; Environmental; Demographic

Sustainability **C.O.P.S. Diamond**

ECONOMY

Sustainability Complementors

Sustainability Market (Demanders)

ECOSYSTEM (Sector; Segment)

"Governors" (Other Parties)

Partners (Suppliers)

Co-creators (Customer)

Profitable Sustainable Org.

Sustainability Competitors (Startups or Insurgents; Substitutors or Incumbents)

Sustainability Industry (Suppliers)

Key = Business Model Strip

= Business Model Canvas

⟷ = Extended Value Chain

The foregoing Shared Value Maps are templates for showing the 4E's (Enterprise; Ecosystem; Economy; Environment) at a given point in time. In other words, those Shared Value Maps are static. Nevertheless, by presenting Shared Value Maps over time we can observe evolution of the 4E's. A **SpaceTime Shared Value Map** is one tool that can be used to present a Shared Value Map at two or more points in time.

SPACETIME SHARED VALUE MAP: Evolution of Business Model

WHEN: Future *(To Do)*/Present *(Doing)*/Past *(Done)*
Stakeholder: ....
Project Goal or Job To Get Done (JTGD): ....
Pain Solving Question (PSQ): How Might We Eliminate Pain (HMWEP) of "X"?
ENVIRONMENT (Context: Local/Global): ....

ECONOMY (*Agriculture/Mining; Manufacturing; Services; Experience Macro-Supply Chain*)			
SPACE *ECOSYSTEM* (*Industry; Market; Competitors; Compl.*)			
ENTERPRISE (*System/Pipe/Platform*): *Business Model Strip/ Business Model Canvas*			
	PAST *(Done)*	*PRESENT* *(Doing)*	*FUTURE* *(To Do)*
		TIME	

A SpaceTime Shared Value Map, which uses a 3x3 "Fractal Grid," can be used to facilitate *Multilevel Business Model Planning and Project Management* and in particular, to answer the 3 basic questions of planning:

o **PAST Shared Value Map:** Where were we (4E's)?

o **PRESENT Shared Value Map:** Where currently are we (4E's)?

o **FUTURE Shared Value Map:** Where must we go (4E's)?

A SpaceTime Shared Value Map has many other uses. For instance, it could be used to develop and manage Strategy as well as a corresponding set of tactics for a startup or an existing organization with a view to winning in the marketplace. When developing strategy, a fourth question should be added to the 3 basic planning questions.

Strategy Question
   o   How best to move from Present to Future (Desired) Shared Value Map: *from Red Ocean Business Model to Blue Ocean Business Model?*

A SpaceTime Map for facilitating the development of strategy is shown below. *A SpaceTime Shared Value Map provides the context of a business model.*

SPACETIME SHARED VALUE MAP: Strategy Planning & Execution

WHEN: Future *(To Do)*/Present *(Doing)*/Past *(Done)*
Stakeholder: ....
Project Goal or Job To Get Done (JTGD): ....
Pain Solving Question (PSQ): How Might We Eliminate Pain (HMWEP) of "X"?
ENVIRONMENT (Context: Local/Global): ....

	Strength/Weakness	*Opportunity/Threat*	
ECONOMY (Agriculture/Mining; Manufacturing; Services; Experience Macro-Supply Chain)			
SPACE *ECOSYSTEM (Industry; Market; Competitors; Compl.)*			
ENTERPRISE (System/Pipe/Platform): Business Model Strip/ Business Model Canvas	*"As Was"* (Gray Ocean) Business Model	*"As Is"* (Red Ocean) Business Model	*"To Be"* (Blue Ocean) Business Model
	PAST (Done)	*PRESENT* (Doing) **TIME**	*FUTURE* (To Do)

STRATEGY →

Although a Business Model Canvas is often presented as a stand-alone document, its structural context is provided by a Business Model Environment map and more comprehensively, by a SpaceTime Shared Value Map. For a startup, future customers come from the ecosystem of the proposed business model. The diagram below illustrates the *multilevel context of a Business Model Canvas, Value Chain, and Business Model Strip.*

SPACETIME SHARED VALUE MAP: *Context of business modeling tools*
Project Goal or Job To Get Done (JTGD): ………..……………
Pain Solving Question (PSQ): How Might We Eliminate Pain (HMWEP) of "X"?
ENVIRONMENT (Context: Local/Global): …………………………

| | *Strength/Weakness* | *Opportunity/Threat* |

ECONOMY
(Agriculture/Mining;
Manufacturing; Services;
Experience
Macro-Supply Chain)

SPACE
ECOSYSTEM
(Industry; Market;
Competitors; Compl.)

ENTERPRISE
(System/Pipe/Platform):
Business Model Strip/
Business Model Canvas/
Value Chain

PAST   *PRESENT*   *FUTURE*
(Done)   *(Doing)*   *(To Do)*
TIME

A key advantage of the SpaceTime Shared Value Map relative to the Business Model Environment is the fractal (modular) 3x3 structure of the former. For a given point in time, rectangular cells or modules can be added on top of a Business Model Canvas or Business Model Strip at the level of the Ecosystem, Economy, and Environment. Also, one can simultaneously consider external constraints when designing or evaluating specific business models at the level of an enterprise. Finally, a SpaceTime Shared Value Map can be used to organize and manage in a multilevel hierarchy a *portfolio of business models* in the past, present, and future.

9 PREDICTABLE DISRUPTION OF THE BUSINESS MODEL CANVAS AND ITS DERIVATIVES: THE POWER OF ZERO TIME, ZERO SPACE (ZTZS) PLATFORMS

Although the term of "business plan," is still more popular than that of "business model," the term of "business model" is rapidly gaining greater popularity. Use of the term "business model" took off during the Internet (dotcom) boom in the early 1990's. However, conception of the term "business model" far precedes that time. A paper by Osterwalder, Pigneur, and Tucci, which was published in 2005, notes that the term "business model" first appeared in 1957 in an academic article by Bellman et al. In time, explicit knowledge regarding business models has progressed from *declarative knowledge* ('knowing WHAT') to *procedural knowledge* ('knowing HOW'). The interdependent relationship between the concept of business plan and business model is becoming clearer. A future business model (diagram, template, or canvas) can be presented as a "one page business plan." However, *present and future business models more fully define a business plan.*

Today, visual tools for directly mapping, documenting, managing, and evaluating business models while reducing pain include the following templates: Value Chain; Strategy Map; Balanced Scorecard; 4 Box Business Model; Business Model Canvas, and Lean Canvas. The Balanced Scorecard and Business Model Canvas are the two most popular tools. However, these two tools are not seamlessly integrated; each virtually exists in its own silo. Nevertheless, the common characteristic among these tools is the use of block diagramming techniques. In short, the most popular templates involve "Fat" Business Modeling tools. With the exception of the Business Model Strip, pure linear diagramming techniques or "Lean" Business Modeling tools are non-existent in the domain of business model visualization.

With regard to the threat of disruption of the Business Model Canvas and its derivative tools, one may ask, "**What business is the Business Model Canvas in?**" It is easy to say that the Business Model Canvas is in the business of Business Model Innovation & Improvement (BMII). Although the response is logically true, that perspective of the Business Model Canvas is too narrow. To take a poetic license from Theodore Levitt, we could say that the aforementioned view suffers from *"Business Modeling Myopia."* For sustainable positioning of the Business Model Canvas, we would have to ask, **"What is the Goal or Job To Get Done (JTGD) of the Business Model Canvas?"** In other words, what "jobs" do people hire the Business Model Canvas to do? Or at best, what pains do people hire the Business Model Canvas to solve?

In practice, the Business Model Canvas is "hired" to do many *pain-solving jobs* in both for-profit organizations and non-profit organizations. Examples of jobs for the Business Model Canvas include the following:

Jobs To Get Done (JTGD) of Business Model Canvas
- o   Map or document a past/present/future business model especially for a given value proposition, strategy, goal, pain-to-be-solved, and/or job to get done
- o   Present how the whole and parts of a business model work
- o   Rapidly design/prototype an innovative business model
- o   Develop a portfolio of (short/medium/long term) business models for sustainable competitive advantage
- o   Translate a business idea, vision, or strategy into a hypothetical business model (project) that can be tested and validated for viability, profitability, and/or sustainability
- o   Provide a common or shared visual language and in particular, a register of topics for describing, discussing, analyzing, and designing business models
- o   Facilitate presentation of an executive summary of a business plan as "one page business plan"
- o   Teach/Explain about the structure of an extended enterprise
- o   Align organization and facilitate shared understanding so that all team members are on the same page of a business model
- o   Align business models during Mergers & Acquisitions events
- o   Rapidly test for problem-solution fit and product-market fit
- o   Explore business models and scenarios for new growth
- o   Restructure existing value chain or business model
- o   Explore business model scenarios for a new career or job

Benefits of using a Business Model Canvas include the following:

Delight of Business Model Canvas
- o   Excellent *visual executive summary on 1 page* of a business plan
- o   Relative brevity in using 9 topics/blocks on one page to describe a business model; cf. classic bulky business plan
- o   Facilitates comparison of business models in many domains
- o   Easy updating especially when sticky notes (Post Its) are used
- o   Easy customization of business modeling topics in domains such as social entrepreneurship and non-profit organizations
- o   Elimination of gap between strategy formulation and execution (experimentation)
- o   Versatility: applicable to many types of project goals
- o   Greater clarity of how existing/new business model works

Weaknesses of the Business Model Canvas are summarized below:

Pain of Business Model Canvas

o Business Model Canvas is a "fat" (block diagram) business modeling tool that does not focus on eliminating pain or answering one or more explicit Pain Solving Questions (PSQ)

o Does not use a Pain Solving Question (PSQ) to rapidly summarize the story or plot of business model or organization

o Rigid visual structure of 9 tessellated building blocks in a fixed configuration of Business Model Canvas; novel visualizations with other cause-and-effect logic and insights are unexplored

o Requires relatively significant amount of money, energy, and time to effectively learn as well as apply; relatively slow tool

o Complexity increases when platforms are being modeled

o No inherent indication of flows or exchange of resources between building blocks; *hidden cause-and-effect logic*

o Inadequate instruction on how to use the Business Model Canvas especially for eliminating pain and/or achieving goals or delight in any domain: physical (body); intellectual (mind); emotional (heart); spiritual (soul)

o *Existing layout of topics is enterprise and product-centric*

o Not optimized for non-profit organizations which inherently have platform business models (2/3-sided markets or multi-stakeholders); each stakeholder should have its own PSQ

o **Neglect of system feedback (sense-and-respond) loop**

o *Neglect of Pain-Plan-Do-Review (PPDR) Cycle as a process for Universal Pain Solving & Project Management*

o Business Model Canvas cannot be described using the back of a standard business card or coin envelope

o Does not use a visual linear template to present the business model of existing or planned organizations; non-obvious link to supply chain-based tools involving value creator & recipient

o Does not present Canvas as part of a *comprehensive visual notation system for business model documentation, analysis, and design*

o Business Model Canvas is not seamlessly integrated with classic tools such as Supply Chain, Value Chain, Balanced Scorecard, and Strategy Map as well as Lean Startup Method

o Not easy to do business model performance management especially using "Innovation Accounting" or dashboards

o Not readily integrated with the visual tool of Business Model Environment; Big picture or context is initially ignored

o Theoretical development of the Business Model Canvas appears to be stagnated; improvements are incremental

Given the above Jobs To Get Done as well as Pain and Delight of the Business Model Canvas, we can say that the Business Model Canvas is in the Business Of Goal Achievement (BOGA) as well as Business Of Pain Solving (BOPS). Both BOGA and BOPS are two sides of the same coin. By framing BOGA/BOPS as the domain of the Business Model Canvas, we can observe its direct and indirect competitors.

One interesting insight is that the Business Model Canvas is competing with tools for Project Planning & Performance Management. This insight highlights opportunities for and threats to growth of the Business Model Canvas as a tool for BOGA/BOPS. An emerging question is: In the near future, would the Business Model Canvas be disrupted as a tool for BOGA/BOPS?

In theory, any real-life tool can be disrupted. Every real-life tool can be disrupted by a Zero Time, Zero Space (ZTZS) platform that provides, at least, similar functionalities as a given tool while minimizing its pain and maximizing its delight using little or no extra use of resources such as money, energy, and time. A "Zero Time (ZT)" tool delivers desired results instantly or on demand. A "Zero Space (ZS)" Tool virtually occupies any physical space; it is a field or exists in digital form. "Zero Time, Zero Space" defines the basic properties of an ideal tool with a given functionality or job to get done or for eliminating pain.

At the moment, the Business Model Canvas is not a Zero Space, Zero Time tool especially as it uses block diagramming techniques. In contrast, the Business Model Strip is close to a Zero Time, Zero Space tool. But can the Business Model Strip disrupt the Business Model Canvas especially in a pain-solving environment that is Volatile, Uncertain, Complex, and Ambiguous (VUCA)?

As noted above, the Business Model Canvas is applicable to a wide variety of Jobs To Get Done. The Business Model Canvas has been instrumental in ushering a phase of business model visualization and planning that focuses on using a common visual template and set of topics (building blocks) for mapping the elements of a business model. With regard to business planning, the Business Model Canvas supports the Lean Startup Method as a 'project scorecard' for documenting and testing hypotheses as well as managing experiments relating to the elements of a proposed or planned business model. However, Osterwalder has **not focused on developing a comprehensive notation system for the Business Model Canvas** so that it can be used as a tool for Universal Pain

Solving & Project Management (UPSPM). And it is in the absence of a notation system for comprehensively carrying out UPSPM that lies the vulnerability of the Business Model Canvas to being disrupted.

Since publication of the Business Model Generation book in 2009, development of the tool of the Business Model Canvas has been incremental and mostly, superficial. *Changes to the Business Model Canvas have hardly increased understanding of how to use the Business Model Canvas for Universal Pain Solving and Project Management.* The Business Model Canvas is mostly used as a visual checklist in startup projects. Changes mostly relate to modifying topics and/or adding cells (building blocks) to the classic Business Model Canvas. The Lean Canvas is one example of a "new" or "bespoke" canvas, the change of which involves modifying topics of the original Business Model Canvas.

In few instances, the shape of the Business Model Canvas is altered but the resulting Canvas functions as a visual checklist of topics for business model visualization. It seems as if academic or theoretical development of the Business Model Canvas has saturated or reached a plateau. Knowledge about the structure and logic of the Business Model Canvas seems to have reached its 'limit of growth.'

The most popular systematic process for using the Business Model Canvas is that advocated by Steve Blank. Using the Business Model Canvas as part of his "Customer Development Stack" while focusing on Lean Startups, Blank advocates using the Business Model Canvas for rapidly documenting and testing hypotheses of a planned business model. The Customer Development Stack consists of three layers or sets of tools: Customer Development Model; Agile (Product) Development Model; Business Model (Logic Diagram). However, Blank does not propose a Pain Solving Question (PSQ) that could be the overarching focus of all tools in his Customer Development Stack. Instead in his co-authored book, "The Startup Owner's Manual," Blank outlines a detailed process for Customer Discovery and Validation that uses the Business Model Canvas as a scorecard.

Using the Business Model Strip with a Pain Solving Question is more efficient and less expensive than learning how to apply the Customer Development process to the Business Model Canvas. The most potent disruptive competitor to Steve Blank's platform or Customer Development Stack is the ("Zero Time, Zero Space") visual platform of the Business Model Strip when used in conjunction with the Pain Solving Question (PSQ): *How Might We Eliminate Pain (HMWEP) of X?*

Below is a set of diagrams and tools that are directly derived from the Business Model Strip. The diagrams focus on the Business Model StripDiamond. All 9 topics of the Business Model Canvas are covered in the Business Model StripDiamond below.

Business Model Strip: One Line Business Model (Showing Topics of Pain-Plan-Do-Review (PPDR) Cycle as well as Kanban Board)

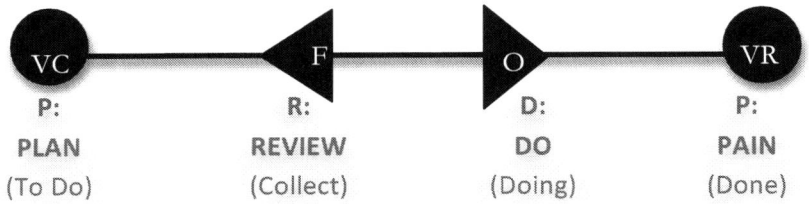

P:	R:	D:	P:
PLAN	**REVIEW**	**DO**	**PAIN**
(To Do)	(Collect)	(Doing)	(Done)

Business Model StripDiamond

Sense-and-Respond Trade Loop

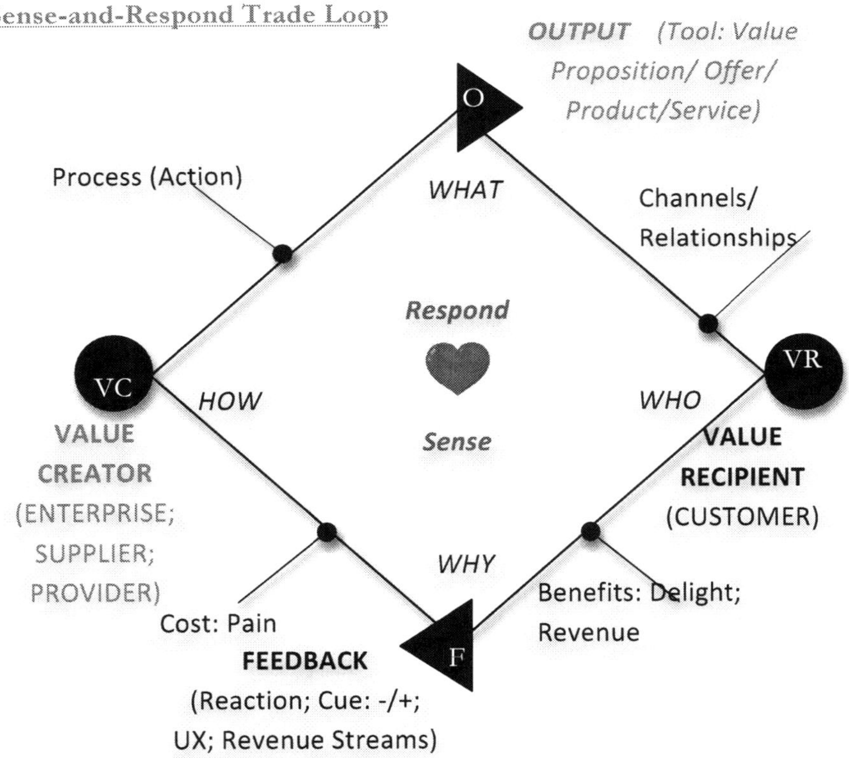

OUTPUT *(Tool: Value Proposition/ Offer/ Product/Service)*

Process (Action)

WHAT

Channels/ Relationships

Respond

VC

HOW

Sense

VR

WHO

VALUE CREATOR
(ENTERPRISE; SUPPLIER; PROVIDER)

VALUE RECIPIENT
(CUSTOMER)

WHY

Benefits: Delight; Revenue

Cost: Pain

FEEDBACK
(Reaction; Cue: -/+; UX; Revenue Streams)

In order to present a less cognitively demanding Business Model StripDiamond, the labels on the legs of the diamond are omitted. Derivative tools ("Children" or "Molecules") of the StripDiamond are subsequently shown.

Business Model StripDiamond: *Excluding labels on legs of diamond*

Sense-and-Respond Trade Loop

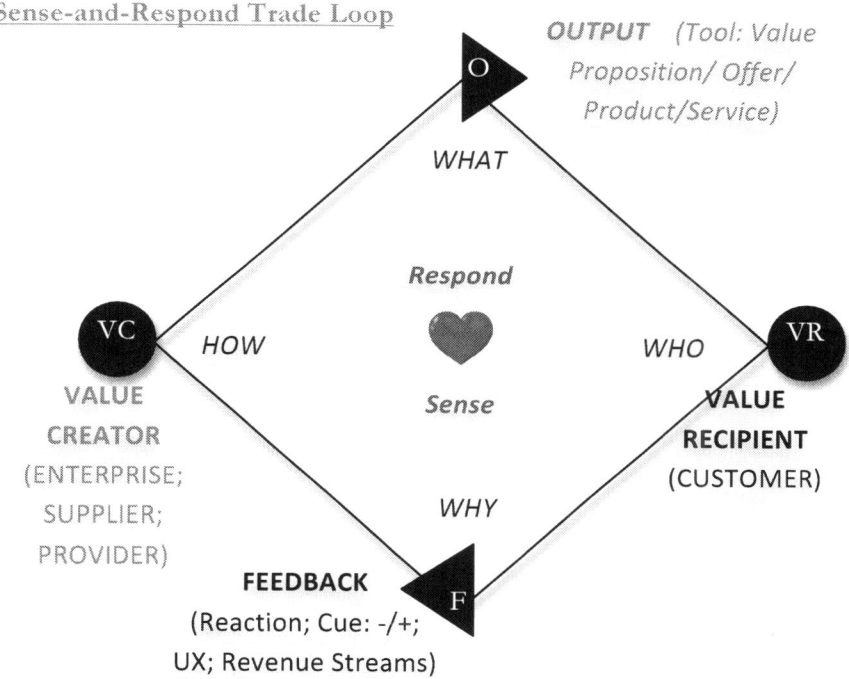

Sense Triangle (ST): WHO-WHY-HOW for Problem (Customer) Discovery & Validation

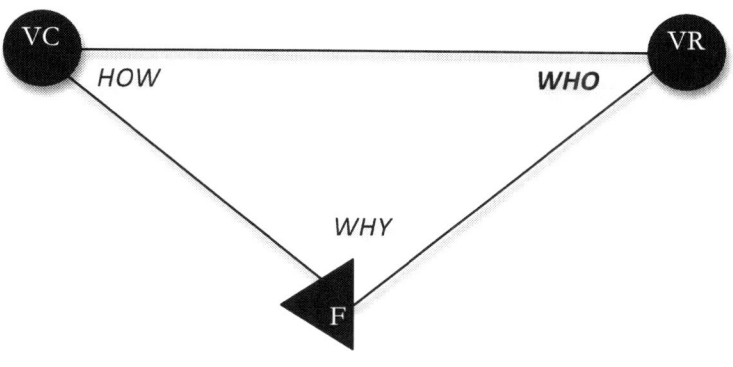

Respond Triangle (RT): WHO-WHAT-HOW for Solution (Product) Discovery & Validation

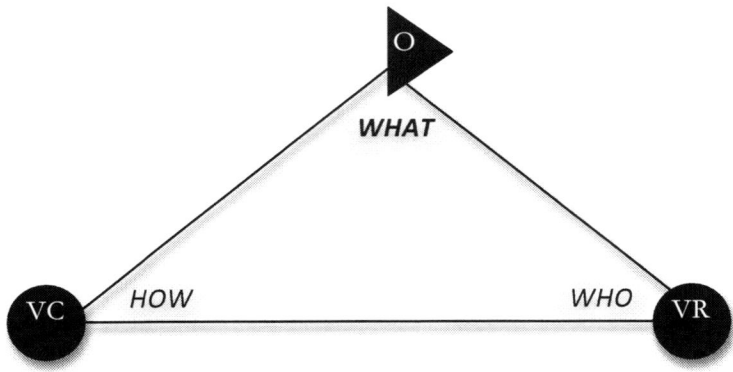

Communication (Golden) Triangle: WHY-HOW-WHAT for Making Inspiring Presentations

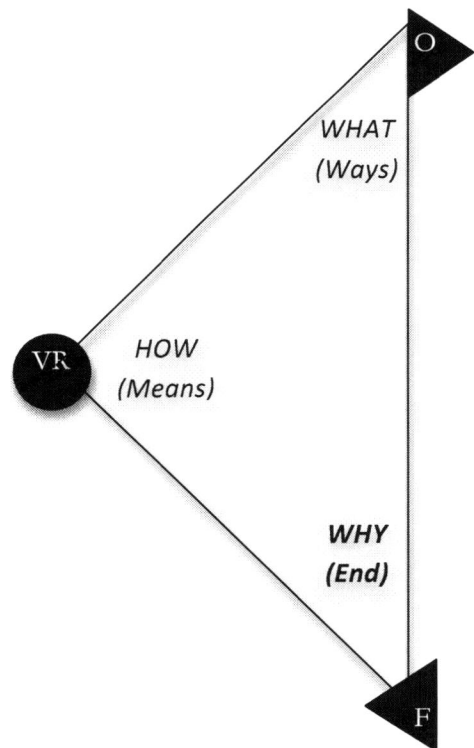

Value Proposition Triangle (VPT) for Value Proposition-Revenue Fit

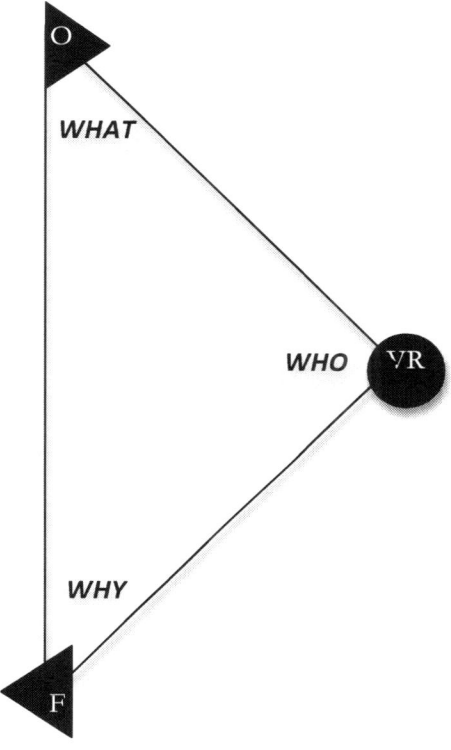

The above triangles show a family of three-node tools that are directly derived from a Business Model Strip. Some of the triangles show topics of well known tools; for instance, the Communication (Golden) Triangle is related to the topics of Simon Sinek's Golden Circle while the Value Proposition Triangle summarizes the essence of Joan Magretta's "Value Proposition Triangle of Questions." These two tools reflect the tip of the iceberg of tools that are directly related to the Business Model StripDiamond. In a Slideshare presentation, I relate over 40 tools to the Business Model Strip Diamond, which is referred to as a 4Q-Diamond; see http://www.slideshare.net/RodKing/simply-standardize-over-30-business-modeling-tools-the-4qbusiness-model-interface . Consequently, the topics of existing tools can be translated into those of the Business Model StripDiamond; vice versa. This property of the Business Model StripDiamond means that it can found the foundation of a common visual language for pain solving and project management especially in business.

The linear layout of a Business Model Strip means that it can easily be related to many linear and tabular tools in and out of business model visualization. Below, a Business Model StripTable is presented in the form of a morphological box: below each heading or topic is a list of different options for that object. Novel business models can be created by (randomly) combining topics from nodes for the Value Creator, Output, Value Recipient, and Feedback. This approach is based on the Morphological Box technique that is used in Creative Problem Solving projects. The "rigid" non-linear structure of the Business Model Canvas prevents users from exploring complementary creativity and innovation techniques such as used in the Morphological Box.

Of all existing tools, no tool has done more for raising the awareness of systematic and visual business modeling than the Business Model Canvas. As pointed out earlier, however, people are so boxed in the paradigm of 9 building blocks that they cannot think out of the box of the Business Model Canvas. This makes the tool and methodology of the Business Model Canvas very vulnerable to being disrupted by a tool such as the Business Model Strip.

If we are using the history of innovation as a guide, the disruption of the Business Model Canvas is predictable at least at a product level. The Business Model Canvas will be disrupted by a Zero Time, Zero Space (ZTZS) tool that is more versatile in application especially for resolving and managing pain in any domain. But, for a disruptive product innovation to be sustainable, it would have to be 'wrapped' in a disruptive or Blue Ocean business model. From the history of disruptive innovations, that would not take place overnight. The process of discovering , validating, and scaling a viable business model takes time. Consequently, the Business Model Canvas has some longevity. In my view, however, the days of the Business Model Canvas are numbered. The Canvas may soon be on 'life support' especially as younger and younger Value Creators become serious entrepreneurs as well as business model disruptors and improvers.

Business Model Strip: One Line Business Model (Showing Topics of Pain-Plan-Do-Review (PPDR) Cycle as well as Kanban Board)

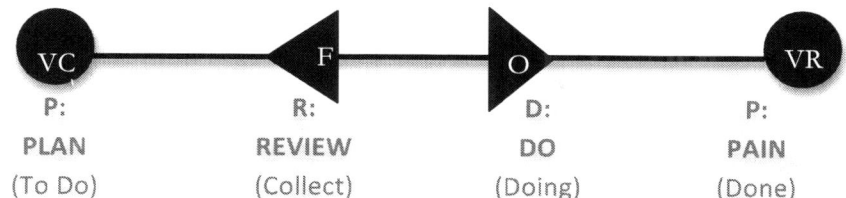

P:	R:	D:	P:
PLAN	REVIEW	DO	PAIN
(To Do)	(Collect)	(Doing)	(Done)

Business Model StripTable 1: *Choices of Elements for a Business Model*
How Might We Eliminate Pain (HMWEP) of X?

VALUE CREATOR (VC)	Feedback (F): Cue (-/+); UX; Revenue	Value Proposition (VP): Offer (Product/Service)	VALUE RECIPIENT (VR)
Low Cost (Strategy)	Asset (Product/ Service) Sale; Free; Vouchers	Product: Non-/ Customizable	Low-end or Mass Market; Long Tail (Automation)
High End or Differentiation (Strategy)	Premium Pricing; Installments; Pre-order	Service; Zero-Space; Zero-Time; On Demand; Do-It-Yourself	High-end/ Luxury/ Exclusive/ Differentiated Market (Customer Intimacy); Ads
Disruptive Innovation (Strategy)	Subscription	Segmented Product: Razor & Blade	Good Enough Experience (Dealers)
Blue Ocean Strategy	Usage	Miniature/Micro-Product	Niche; Community
Pipe/Platform	Licensing	Auction; Un/Bundled	Two-sided Market
Infrastructure	Brokerage; Royalties	Offline/Online; Modular	Three-sided Market
Outsourcing; Contractors	Lending/Leasing	Elegant/Beautiful	Face-to-Face Experience
Production/ Manufacturing	Auction	Cheap/Low Frills/Free	Automation Experience
Problem Solving	Freemium	High Functionali-ty/Performance	Direct/ Disintermediation
Partners/ Alliances	Pay What You Want	Simple/ Convenient	Do It Yourself (Self Service

Business Model Strip Table 2: *Choices of Elements for a Business Model*
How Might We Eliminate Pain (HMWEP) of X?

VALUE CREATOR (VC)	Feedback (F): Cue (-/+); UX; Revenue	Value Proposition (VP): Offer (Product/Service)	VALUE RECIPIENT (VR)
Co-creation/ Open Innovation/ Collaboration	Crowdfunding	Add-on (Ancillary/ Peripheral) Product/Service	End Customer
Crowdsourc-ing	Barter	Cross-selling	Intermediate Customer
Demand Leveling		Emotional/ Multisensory Experience: *Adventure; Beauty; Self-expression*	End Consumer
Platform or Infrastruc-ture as Service		Discounted Product/Service	Prosumer
Integrator		Guaranteed Availability	Lock-in
Open Source		Minimum Viable Product; No Frills	Long-tail Market
Orchestrator		Product as Service	Poor/Needy/ Bottom of Pyramid
Performance-based Contracting		Shared Service	Automation Experience
Reverse Engineering		White Label Goods	Early Adopters/ Evangelists
Reverse Innovation		Virtual Goods	Brand Ambassadors
		Values-based or Cause-driven Proposition	
		Nostalgia-based Proposition	

10 WHY EVERY VALUE CREATOR NEEDS TO INSTANTLY UNDERSTAND AND USE THE VISUAL LANGUAGE OF OPEN & MULTILEVEL PAIN SOLVING

"Every Built-To-Last Organization is a Rapid & Continuous Value Creator."

Every day, the world is getting more complex and difficult to understand as well as predict. Due to a globally networked economy, the *environment is more Volatile, Uncertain, Complex, and Ambiguous (VUCA).* Pain is therefore unexpectedly popping and affecting enterprises everywhere.

Shared Value Map for VUCA Environment: 3D-   Dashboard
WHERE:

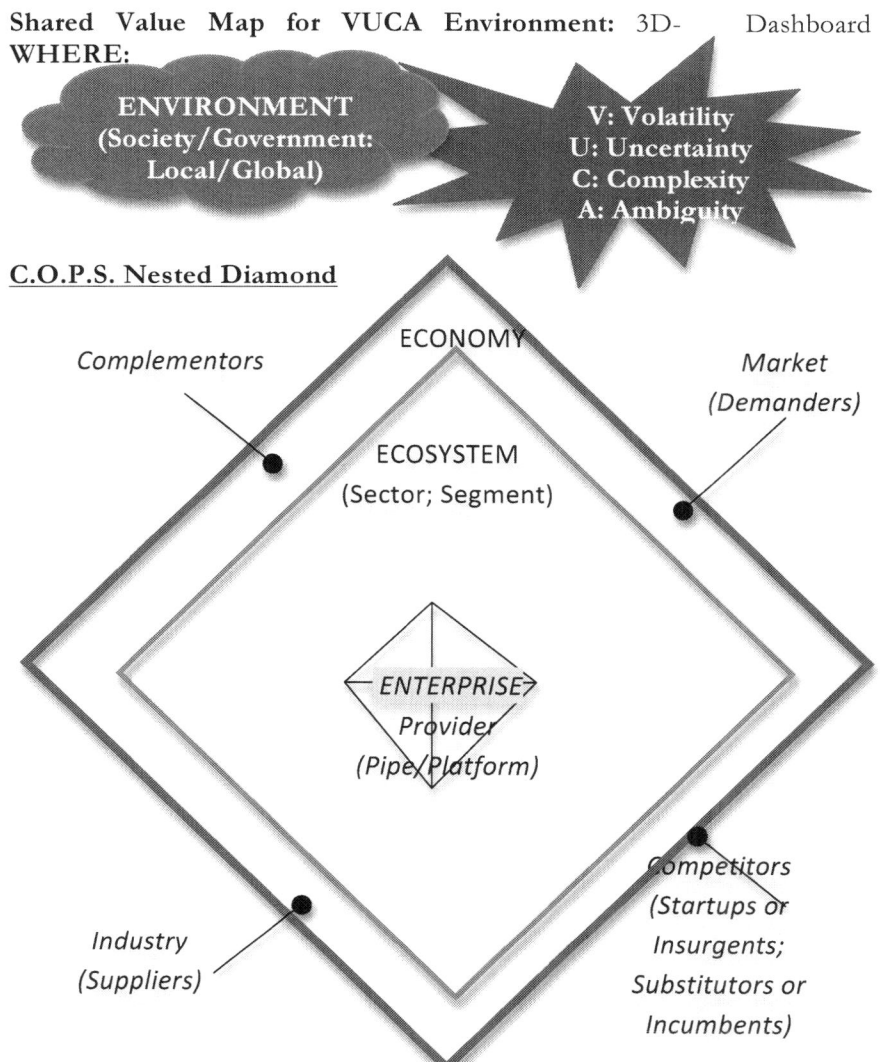

ENVIRONMENT
(Society/Government:
Local/Global)

V: Volatility
U: Uncertainty
C: Complexity
A: Ambiguity

C.O.P.S. Nested Diamond

Complementors

ECONOMY

Market
(Demanders)

ECOSYSTEM
(Sector; Segment)

←ENTERPRISE→
Provider
(Pipe/Platform)

Industry
(Suppliers)

Competitors
(Startups or
Insurgents;
Substitutors or
Incumbents)

Actually, there is VUCA as well as chaos and emergent pain at the level of the 4 E's: Environment; Economy, Ecosystem; Enterprise. Making sense of today's world and deeply understanding its pains requires a pain solving language that differentiates and recognizes the 4E's. In the business Model Generation book, only two levels are distinguished: Business Model Level (Canvas) and Business Model Environment. For a multilevel strategy for resolving pain, or trade-offs, the 4E levels are required. A Value Engine Map facilitates multilevel pain solving as well as strategy formulation and management. An example of a Value Engine Map is presented below.

Value Engine Map: Business Model Pipes/Platforms in Health Care

Time: *Past (Done)/Present (Doing)/Future (To Do)*

Goal or Job To Get Done: Instantly Improve Value of Healthcare

Environment (Context; Location): ....
PSQ: *How Might We Eliminate Pain (HMWEP) of X?*
Ideal Value Prop. (IVP): *Highest Quality of Healthcare at Zero Cost*

High	Online & Lean Pain/Disease/ Wellness Management Network; Telemedicine *(Pipe/Platform)*	Specialized Physician Practice/ Clinic *(Pipe)*	Highly Specialized Hospital: Heart; Stroke; Eye; etc. *(Pipe/Platform: Coupled)*
DELIGHT (+): Quality *(Performance)* — *Moderate*	Specialty Physician/Clinic *(Pipe)* Retail Clinic *(Platform: Uncoupled)*	**General Physician Practice/ Clinic** *(Platform: Uncoupled)*	**General Hospital/ Multispecialty Clinic** *(Platform: Unc/Coupled)*
Low			

"TAME" PAIN	*Moderate*	"WICKED" PAIN
(Acute; Simple; Routine)		*(Chronic; Complex)*

PAIN (-): Cost *(Time)*

In the preceding paragraphs, I talked about the emergence of pain everywhere. Pain, especially in the form of greater entropy or constraints, is the common denominator of living systems and organizations. Despite the commonality of pain, there is currently no standard process for resolving pain. Perhaps, in no sector is this lack of a common language for pain solving necessary than in the health care system especially in the USA. In the health care system, the proverbial *Tower of Babel* seems to be at work.

In the book, "The Innovator's Prescription," Clayton Christensen et al write:

"Almost every day somewhere in the United States, a group of health-care reformers convenes a conference. We've attended many of these. Nearly without exception the participants talk past each other. This one focuses on the uninsured poor, that one on prescription coverage for the elderly, another on overuse of expensive diagnostics technology, and still someone else on the cost of end-of-life care. Someone decries the perversions of fee-for-service reimbursement, while someone else bewails the failings of capitation.

Christensen et al add:

"They [reformers] talk past one another because they don't share a common language and a common understanding of the root cause of these problems. Unable to agree on the problem, and without a language for understanding one another, they find it impossible to articulate and agree upon promising solutions."

Given the growing crisis in health care especially in the USA, the following paragraphs use health care as an example for presenting visual tools of a common language for Standard Pain Solving & Project Management (SPSPM). The presented visual tools are applicable to other sectors of the economy. Having a shared language for reducing and managing pain would help to rapidly reduce cost and time as well as increase quality and performance in projects. Instead of a lot of "blah-blah-blah" in meetings, members of a team can use the same suite of visual tools to better communicate and collaborate while achieving a shared vision.

The paradigm of multilevel pain solving drives the methodology of Standard Pain Solving & Project Management. Lack of multilevel pain solving may be at the root of problems in health care especially in the USA. A Shared Value Map can be used to present a hierarchy of problems.

Alternatively, the problems or pains can be listed according to the 4E's: Environment; Economy; Ecosystem; Enterprise. Below, the 4E Hierarchy is used to present existing "pains" of the health care system in the USA. The source of information is two fold: from Christensen et al's book, "The Innovator's Prescription.as well as Porter et al's "Redefining Health Care."

4E-Multilevel Hierarchy: Existing Pain in Health Care System (USA)

4E-MULTILEVEL HIERARCHY	DESCRIPTION OF SITUATION: PAIN
Environment (Society)	▪ *More and more people including the elderly, retirees, and uninsured families in society do not have access to medical care* ○ *Health care costs in the US are among the highest in the world even though many citizens do not have health coverage*
Economy (Government/ Supply Chain)	▪ *Health Care Spending is rising faster than rate of growth of GDP; Health Care Spending occupies a large share of National Budget.* ▪ *Inadequate funds for investment in technical infrastructure.* ▪ *Large government liability regarding provision of health care to retired employees* ▪ *Regulators do not facilitate business model innovation* ○ *Reforms have failed to resolve trade-offs in health care: reformers have tended to focus on a single issue or problem that must be addressed*
Ecosystem (Health Care Sector/ Industry)	▪ *Unsustainable cost structure: rising cost vs. restricted (inaccessible) health services as well as lower quality* ○ *Failure of Competition in Health Care: high cost; unsatisfactory quality; limited access to health care* ○ *Players strive not to create value for patients but to capture more revenue, shift costs, and restrict services; priority on quantity, not on quality*
Enterprise (Business Model)	• *Lack of business model innovation: "bundled" business model of general hospitals is inefficient and costly* • *Rising cost for employers, employees, and retirees* ○ *Enterprises are not engaged in value-based competition for results; patients are over-treated*

A simplified version of a 4E-Multilevel Hierarchy over time is shown below as a SpaceTime Shared Value Map.

SPACETIME SHARED VALUE MAP: *Shared Value Dashboard* **(SVD)** *for Health Care Industry*
WHEN: Future *(To Do)*/Present *(Doing)*/Past *(Done)*
Stakeholder: ....
Project Goal or Job To Get Done (JTGD): *Ideal (Universal) Healthcare*
Pain Solving Question (PSQ): How Might We Eliminate Pain (HMWEP) of "X"?
ENVIRONMENT (Context: Local/Global): *P.E.S.T.L.I.E.D.*
Value (Feedback): *Strength/Weakness Opportunity/Threat*

	PAST (Done)	PRESENT (Doing)	FUTURE (To Do)
ECONOMY *(Agriculture/Mining; Manufacturing; Services; Experience Macro-Supply Chain)*	Past Economy	Real-time News/Statistics/Data on * **Service** Sector of Economy: Health (Non-customers)	Future Economy *(Predictions/ Scenarios)*
SPACE *ECOSYSTEM* *(Industry; Market; Competitors; Compl.)*	Past Healthcare Ecosystem *(Forces; Value Net)*	*** Existing Healthcare Ecosystem** *(Forces): Analogs; Antilogs*	*Future Healthcare Ecosystem *(Forces; Value Net)*
ENTERPRISE *(System/Pipe/Platform): Business Model Strip/ Business Model Canvas/ Value Chain*		BLUE OCEAN STRATEGY (E.R.I.C.: Eliminate; Reduce; Increase; Create) TACTICS: PPDR Cycle	
	"*As Was*" *(Gray Ocean) Business Model*	"*As Is*" *(Red Ocean) Business Model -* Core Values	"*To Be*" *(Blue Ocean) Business Model –* Vision/ Mission

PAST *(Done)*	PRESENT *(Doing)*	FUTURE *(To Do)*

TIME

We can see from the 4E-Multilevel Hierarchy for Pain that the health care problem is not just a technology (enterprise level) or regulatory (economy level) problem. The health care problem is not even solely a business model (enterprise level) or a value-based competition (economy/industry) problem. Rather, the health care problem exists at many levels. So, solving the health care problem requires a coordinated and coherent program of multilevel strategies, business models (pipes/ platforms), and projects especially for resolving the trade-off of Quality vs. Cost.

In this book, we focus on the level of the enterprise and ecosystem. The economy and environment are considered to be "severe" external constraints. Relevant tools from the Business Model Generation book are therefore the Business Model Canvas (for enterprise level) and Business Model Environment (for ecosystem level). The question then is:
How Might We Eliminate the Pain (HMWEP) of "X" in the Health Care System while using the tool of the Business Model Canvas and/or Business Model Environment?

Many descriptions and examples of business models are contained in the Business Model Generation book. However, there is no comprehensive taxonomy or classification system ifor categorizing business models. Rather, the book presents a table of five Business Model "Patterns:" *Long Tail* Business Models; *Unbundled* Business Models; *Multi-sided* Platforms; *Free/mium* Business Models; *Open* Business Models. The aforementioned descriptions reflect the unique building block or "epicenter" of a described business model pattern as follows: *Long Tail* (Customer Segments); *Unbundled* (Customer Segments); *Multi-sided* (Customer Segments); *Freemium* (Revenue Streams); *Open* (Key Partners).

While it is interesting to note the characteristics of the above archetypal business models, the categories are not mutually exclusive. For instance, Long Tail business models are inherently platforms and multisided. In fact, all the presented examples in the book deal with platforms that are either two- or multii-sided. There is no example, pattern, or archetype that refers to a company with a single-sided market. Using Osterwalder et al's business model patterns leads to an ambiguous as well as incomplete classification of business models in health care.

A more comprehensive system for classifying business models is provided by Christensen et al who use a typology of three business models: *Solution Shop (SS)* Business Model; *Value-Adding Process (VAP)* Business Model; *Facilitated Network (FN)* Business Model. The main features of each model are presented in the table below.

Classification System for Business Models According to Type of Pain (Tame/Wicked Problem)
How Might We Eliminate Pain (HMWEP) of X?

FORM (Shape)	PIPE	PLATFORM	
BUSINESS MODEL PERSPECTIVE **FUNCTION/PROCESS** (Economy/Supply Chain)	1-Sided Customer Segment: *Chain*	2-Sided Customer Segment: *Valley*	Multi-sided Customer Segment: *Network*
AGRICULTURE/ MINING/EXTRACTION INDUSTRY	* Petroleum Refinery **VALUE-ADDING PROCESSOR**		
MANUFACTURING/ PROCESSING INDUSTRY (Product-Logic and Language of Classic *Value Chain*)	(Acute, Routine, or "Tame" Pain (Problem); Itemized ("Product") Fee: *Outcome-based*); Quality of output or "body repair/surgery" can be standardized and guaranteed) **Examples** * Manufacturer: *Automobile* * Restaurant; Retail * Educational Institutions *** Medical Procedures/Surgery:** *Heart; Eye; Hernia; Knee/Hip*		
SERVICE INDUSTRY (Service-Logic and Language of *Problem (Pain) Diagnosis/Analysis & Prescriptions/Conceptual Solutions*)	**SOLUTION-IDEA SHOP** (cf. Lean Startup) (Complex Symptoms/ Unstructured or "Wicked" Pain (Problem); Highly Trained/Cross-functional Experts; "Advisory" Solutions; Service Fee: *Time-based*) **Examples** * Management Consulting *Ad Agencies * R & D * Law Firms *** Medical:** *Schizophrenia; Epilepsy; Alzheimer's*	**FACILITATED NETWORK** (Chronic Pain; Membership Fee; Fee) **Examples** * Telco * Insurance * Auction/Stock Exchange * Social Network ***Medical:** *Chronic Back Pain; Diabetes; Obesity; Addictions; Chron's Disease*	

Christensen et al's typology of business models is adapted from the work of Stabell and Fjeldstad who first published their business model framework in a paper, "Configuring Value for Competitive Advantage: On Chains, Shops and Networks." Stabell and Fjeldstad primarily differentiated business models according to type of problem, pain, key activity (process), or value creation logic. They originally used the terms of Value Shop and Value Network. In Christensen et al's work, three categories are used: Solution Shop, Value-Adding Process, and Facilitated Network. Value Shop and Solution Shop are synonymous. So are Value Network and Facilitated Network. Value-Adding Process is analogous to Value Chain.

Christensen et al note that "Solution Shops (SS)" are organizations or business models that are structured to diagnose and solve unstructured problems (illnesses). In health care, unstructured illnesses are observed as complex symptoms of unwellness that have unknown, non-obvious, or indeterminate root-causes. Consequently, such unwellness first requires technology assisted diagnostics such as in diagnostic imaging technology and molecular diagnostics. If precise diagnosis and therapy cannot be achieved – such as in a "wicked" problem or pain – then, experimentation and pattern recognition techniques may be applied under the paradigm of intuitive and/or empirical medicine. Solution Shops do not do body repair or surgery. Their focus is on diagnosis and/or prescription for treatment of illness. Increasingly, Solution Shops are focusing on wellness rather than just diagnosing and prescribing for treatment of illness. Solution Shop business models are generally service-focused and charge time-based fees.

A Value-Adding Process (VAP) organization or business model deals with structured, routine, or "tame" problems (illnesses). VAP organizations focus on treating acute or routine pain. Many VAP business models deal with standardized or routine "body repair/surgery:" the quality of an existing body part is improved (or sometimes, the body part is replaced or removed). In contrast to Solution Shops, which charge based on direct inputs such as time, VAP organizations have (fixed) price lists for desired outputs or outcomes.

Facilitated Network (FN) organizations or business models focus on long-term care and in particular, the sharing of information for managing chronic pain, illnesses, or diseases such as in diabetes, obesity, and chronic back pain. Modification of habits or behavior is often required for patients with chronic illnesses. Facilitated Network organizations facilitate interactions especially between members of a given community of patients & families.. Their revenue streams include subscription fees. Presented below is a summary of the features of the three types of business models.

Business Model Strip for Health Care System in the USA

HEALTH CARE	Revenue;	*Health Care*	Population:
PROVIDER:	Benefits; User	*Service*	* Well
* *Hospitals*	Experience (-/+)	*(Product/*	
* *Clinics*		*Medicine)*	* Unwell
* *Physicians*			

VC —◀ F ▶ O — VR

P:	R:	D:	P:
PLAN	REVIEW	DO	PAIN
(To Do)	(Collect)	(Doing)	(Done)

Typology of Business Models: Solution Shop; VAP; Facilitated Network

How Might We Eliminate Pain (HMWEP) of X?
Multi-Business Model Typology *for Health Care Delivery*

VALUE CREATOR (VC) ... *Type/Chain of Bus. Model/ "Job"*	Feedback (F): Cue (-/+); UX; Revenue	Value Proposition (VP): Offer *(Product/Service)*	VALUE RECIPIENT (VR)
SOLUTION-IDEA SHOP – *Measure/Diagnose/ Hypothesize/Solve Unstructured Pain*	Service Fee: *High price (Input-based)* ➤ Intuitive Medicine	Discovery of Pain/Illness/Sick/ Unwellness: *In-patient/Mobile/ Remote (Tele)*	Patient with Symptoms: * *Physical Exam* * *Imaging* * *Monitoring*
VALUE-ADDED PROCESSOR – *Repair, Treat, or Transform Pain of "Defective" Body Part (Whole)*	"Product "Fee: *Lower Price (Output-based or Outcome-based)* ➤ Empirical/ Precision Medicine	Treatment/Cure of Painful or "Defective" Body Part: *In-patient/Mobile/ Remote (Tele)*	Patient with Acute Pain: * *Eye* * *Hernia* * *Heart* * *Bone*
FACILITATED NETWORK – *Exchange/Interact; Prevent/Manage Information (Using Infrastructure)*	Service Fee Subscription/ Membership Fee	Prevent Pain/ Illness/Sickness; Manage Chronic/ Terminal Pain; Keep Well or Fit; Be Happier	Patient:/Family with Chronic Pain: * *Diabetes* Well People

To facilitate documentation and presentation of existing business models in any health care organization, a template for a Business Model StripTable is presented. Provision is made for describing each type of business model.

Business Model Strip for Health Care System

HEALTH CARE PROVIDER: * Hospitals * Clinics * Physicians	Revenue; Benefits; User Experience (-/+)	*Health Care Service (Product/ Medicine)*	Population: * Well * Unwell

VC	F	O	VR
P: **PLAN** (To Do)	R: **REVIEW** (Collect)	D: **DO** (Doing)	P: **PAIN** (Done)

Business Model StripTable: *Performance*

How Might We Eliminate Pain (HMWEP) of X?
Multi-Business Model Typology (Macro-Value Chain)

VALUE CREATOR (VC) ... *Types/Chain of Business Models*	Feedback (F): Cue (-/+); UX; Revenue	Value Proposition (VP): Offer (Product/Service)	VALUE RECIPIENT (VR)
SOLUTION-IDEA SHOP			
VALUE-ADDED PROCESSOR			
FACILITATED NETWORK			

The "atomic" business models of Solution Shops, Value-Adding Process, and Facilitated Network are useful for describing, classifying, and recognizing the business model of every organization especially in the health sector. Organizations have either an "atomic" business model (which could be a solution shop, value-adding process, or facilitated network) or a "bundled" business model (which combines two or more atomic business models). General hospitals are "multi-pain" platforms with bundled business models that involve solution (diagnostic/prescription) shops and value-adding (body repair/surgery) processes.

A Specialist Hospital such as for heart, eye, or knee surgery can be described as a "mono-acute/chronic pain" pipe with a Value-Adding Process business model. There are also Specialist Hospitals that offer a Solution Shop business model for a single chronic pain such as asthma; such a Specialist Hospital would be described as having a "mono-chronic" pipe business model. A Specialist Hospital can have a multi-disciplinary team of doctors working on a specific pain. In contrast, a General Physician's Practice has a single doctor using a "multi-acute-pain" platform with a Solution Shop business model.

With regard to the elements of a business model, Christensen et al list the following four components or "boxes": Value Proposition; Resources; Processes; Profit Formula. These components are related to the Business Model Strip as shown below.

Business Model Strip: Christensen's 4 Elements of a Business Model *(Shown in Conjunction with the Pain-Plan-Do-Review (PPDR) Cycle)*

o **Resources**

o **Processes**

o **Profit Formula**

o **Value Proposition** (Product/ Service)

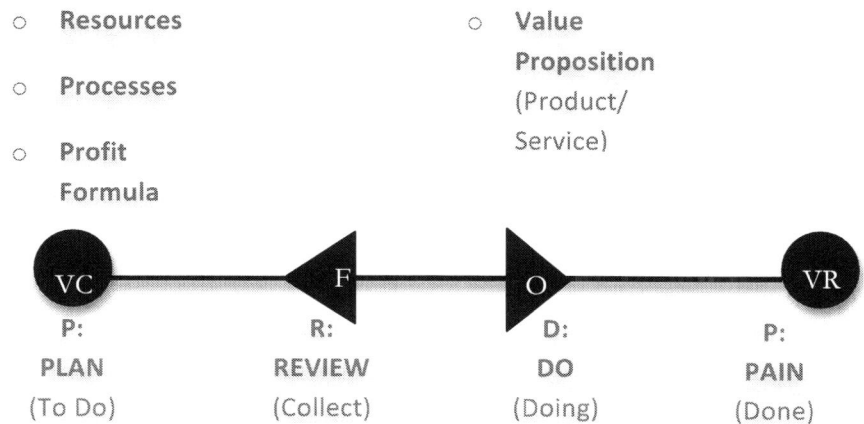

VC	F	O	VR
P:	R:	D:	P:
PLAN	REVIEW	DO	PAIN
(To Do)	(Collect)	(Doing)	(Done)

It is important to note that Christensen's 4 component or 4-Box Business Model is not used as a visual template to illustrate how a specific Solution Shop, Value-Adding Process, or Facilitated Network works. Rather descriptions in the book, *"The Innovation's Prescription,"* are textual and are at a high level of abstraction. No "map" is provided on a health care provider's activities for delivering services to patients. This approach contrasts that of Porter & Teisberg who introduce the tool of "Care Delivery Value Chain." The table below shows the relationship between activities of the Care Delivery Value Chain, Typology of Business Models, Pain-Plan-Do-Review (PPDR) Cycle of the Community Happiness Canvas, and five steps of the Business Model Design Process.

Business Model Design Process for *Health Care Delivery*

Value Chain for Health Care Delivery: Topics/Questions *(Elements of Value Chain)*	Community Happiness Canvas: Topics *(Pain-Plan-Do-Review (PPDR) Cycle)*
SUPPORT ACTIVITIES SOLUTION SHOP o **Informing** o **Measuring** o **Accessing** PRIMARY ACTIVITIES SOLUTION SHOP o **Monitoring/Preventing** o **Diagnosing** VALUE-ADDING PROCESS o **Preparing** o **Intervening** o **Recovering/Rehabilitating** FACILITATED NETWORK o **Monitoring/Managing** (Back end)	MOBILIZE **(PSQ):** *How Might We Eliminate Pain (HMWEP) of "X"?* 1.**UNDERSTAND** (Collect; *Empathize; Define)* 1.1 **Problem/Challenge/Pain** 1.2 Customers/Stakeholders 1.3 **Other Solutions** 2. **DESIGN** (To Do: **Ideas**; *Ideate)* 2.1 Proposed Solution (End) 2.2 Plan of Action (Ways) 2.3 Resources (Means) 3. **IMPLEMENT** (Doing: **Build/ Prototype; Measure;** *Test)* 4. **MANAGE** (Done: **Learn**; Innovation Accounting) 4.1 Budget: COST (STRUCTURE) 4.2 Motivation: BENEFITS – REVENUE (STREAMS)

From the preceding table, we can say that the process for the Care Delivery Value Chain mirrors the "Business Model Chain" of Solution Shops, Value-Adding Processes, and Facilitated Networks. Each chain reflect the universal pain solving process of the PPDR Cycle: Pain (Understand); Plan (Design); Do (Design); Review (Manage). The language of the PPDR Cycle or Business Model Design Process can therefore be used in conjunction with the 'scorecard' of the Business Model Strip and activities of the Care Delivery Value Chain o rapidly improve or innovate on business models in health care. In the Business Model Generation book, there is no explicit link between the Business Model Canvas, Business Model Design Process, and primary activities for health care delivery.

In general, business models in health care are inherent platforms since patients do not directly and personally pay all the bill for their medical costs. Medical bills are usually paid through employer's insurance with Insurers. Consequently, multiple stakeholders are involved in business models in the health care sector. But, who are the stakeholders?
.

There are so many stakeholders in health care that it is a daunting task to keep track of them. However, for effective and efficient delivery of health care, all stakeholders must be identified and known. I have found it useful to organize stakeholders into four categories: Customers; Other Parties; Providers; Suppliers. These categories can be easily remembered as they form an acronym, "COPS."

The COPS stakeholders can be presented at each level of a 4E-hierarchy: Enterprise; Ecosystem; Economy; Environment. A brief description of COPS stakeholders is as follows:

➢ C: Customers (Patient; Value Recipient)
➢ O: Other Parties
➢ P: Provider (Enterprise; Value Creator)
➢ S: Suppliers

The Business Model Canvas is optimized for two categories of stakeholders: Provider (Enterprise; Value Creator) and Customers (Patient; Value Recipient). Color-coding on the Business Model Canvas becomes unwieldy and confusing to read when other stakeholders are added to a Business Model Canvas. Consequently, it is challenging to use the Business Model Canvas in health care which typically has multiple stakeholders. As mentioned earlier, every health care organization is inherently a platform.

Although COPS categories of stakeholders may be listed or presented using a linear format, non-linear formats can be used. Inspired by the "diamond template" to present a group of four in the business literature, I present the COPS Categories using a 3x3 Fractal Grid while maintaining a diamond format as well as the structure of a supply chain. The configuration is shown below in the COPS Fractal Grid.

C.O.P.S. Fractal Grid (3x3): Multilevel Supply Chain or 3E-Business Modeling at a Given Point in Time

WHEN: Future *(To Do)*/Present *(Doing)*/Past *(Done)*
Stakeholder: ....
Project Goal or Job To Get Done (JTGD): *Ideal (Universal) Healthcare*
Pain Solving Question (PSQ): How Might We Eliminate Pain (HMWEP) of "X"?
ENVIRONMENT (Context: Local/Global): ....

	O: **Other Parties**	
S: **Suppliers**	o ECONOMY o ECOSYSTEM o ENTERPRISE	C: **Customers**
	P: **Provider**	

One advantage of using a 3x3 Fractal Grid is its modular structure which lends itself to items being written on modular (index) cards or sticky notes. Team members can therefore work independently on a specific group of stakeholders and later put together the modules in order to see the big picture. At the same time, the "white spaces" of the 3x3 Fractal Grid can be used to accommodate additional notes and information on stakeholders. Subsequent presentations focus on the COPS diagram at the level of the enterprise, ecosystem, and economy.

C.O.P.S. Fractal Grid (3x3): Healthcare Stakeholders at *Enterprise Level*

PSQ: *How Might We Eliminate Pain (HMWEP) of X?*

	O: **Other Parties** (PAYERS) * Employers/Employees * Primary Insurance Payer * Home Health Service * External Caregivers * Med. Association/Unions * Health & Human Services; NGO's: IT Firms; Alliances	
S: **Suppliers** * Drug/Biotech Manufacturers * Equipment/ Device Manufacturers * Pharmacies * Physicians * Med Schools * Nursing Schools	**ENTERPRISE** (Platform) STAKEHOLDERS	C: **Customers** (END USERS) **VALUE RECIPIENT:** * Patients * Family Members * Channels * Customer Relationships
PAIN (-) COST STRUCURE COST *(Time)*	P: **Provider** ⬦ o ENTERPRISE **VALUE CREATOR:** **(General) Hospital** * Doctors/Physicians * Nurses * Administrative Staff * Activities/Processes/ Services/Jobs *for "Body Care"* * Lab (Blood; Xray; etc.) * Equipment/Machinery * Facilities/Resources	*DELIGHT (+)* *REVENUE STREAMS* *BENEFIT* *(Quality)*

The structure of the COPS Fractal Grid at the enterprise level is similar to that of the Shared Value Map at enterprise level. Two main differnces exist between the two types of diagrams. The first is that a Shared Value Map shows all levels of the 4E-Hierarchy while a COPS Fractal Grid typically focuses on one level. Another difference is that flows of P.I.G.S. (Product; Information; Goods; Services) are not indicated between stakeholders in a COPS Fractal Grid. In short, the COPS Fractal Grid presents a visual and static list of stakeholders while a Shared Value Map illustrates a dynamic system at multiple levels. Nevertheless, a COPS Fractal Grid can be transformed into a Shared Value Map; vice versa.

C.O.P.S. Fractal Grid (3x3): Healthcare Stakeholders at *Ecosystem Level*

PSQ: *How Might We Eliminate Pain (HMWEP) of X?*

	O: **Other Parties** COMPETITORS COMPLEMENTORS	
S: **Suppliers** **INDUSTRY**	**ECOSYSTEM** (Value Net/Network; Competitive Forces: *Bargaining Powers &* *Threats*) PLAYERS	C: **Customers** **MARKET** CUSTOMER SEGMENT
PAIN (-) COST STRUCURE COST *(Time)*	P: **Provider** ◈ INDUSTRY SUB-GROUP	*DELIGHT (+)* *REVENUE* *STREAMS* *BENEFIT* *(Quality)*

114

To create effective and efficient strategies for health care, strategies and business models must be developed with a multilevel perspective. The COPS Fractal Grid below shows stakeholders or players at the level of an economy.

C.O.P.S. Fractal Grid (3x3): Healthcare Stakeholders at *Economy Level*

PSQ: *How Might We Eliminate Pain (HMWEP) of X?*

	O: **Other Parties** **GOVERNMENT** **NON-PROFIT ORGANIZATIONS**	
S: **Suppliers** **EXTRACTIVE (Agriculture/ Mining) ECONOMY** **MANUFACTU-RING ECONOMY** **SERVICE ECONOMY**	PLAYERS IN **ECONOMY** (Supply Chain)	C: **Customers** **MARKET** **EXPERIENCE SOCIETY**
PAIN (-) COST STRUCURE COST *(Time)*	P: **Provider** ⬦ SERVICE SUB-GROUP	*DELIGHT (+)* *REVENUE STREAMS* *BENEFIT (Quality)*

11. CONCLUSION & RECOMMENDATION

This book poses the fundamental question, **"Is the Business Model Canvas a good tool with bad instructions?"** So, after focusing on different aspects of this question in 11 chapters, what's the verdict?

In order to answer the above question, it is important to know the frame of reference, context, or expectation regarding the tool of the Business Model Canvas. The Business Model Generation book positions the Business Model Canvas as a 'visual scorecard' for documenting new or existing (pipe) business models. However, for me, that *scorecard* use of the Canvas is too narrow. The essence of the Canvas is more than that. The Canvas can be used as a **multilevel system map** especially for document-ing, analyzing, designing, and managing *"Exponential Organizations."*

As a tool that maps the structure of any extended system or enterprise, the Business Model Canvas has a wide variety of applications regarding pain solving in organizations. Consequently, the Business Model Canvas can and should be elevated to a tool for **Open & Multilevel Pain Solving (OMPS)**. Some people may still ask, "Why expand the scope of use of the Business Model Canvas?" Well, like in nature, business tools need to adapt to the needs of their environment or emerging jobs to get done, otherwise they risk obsolescence, if not death or extinction.

With regard to use of the Business Model Canvas, three categories of customer segments can be identified: Financial Investors; Scalable Startups; Value Creators. The Business Model Canvas must be aligned with the jobs that these multi-stakeholders need to get done. Below is a list of *potential* Jobs To Get Done for each of the aforementioned category of customers.

❖ **Financial Investors:** *Venture Capitalist; Banker; Financier/Sponsor*
- o Rapidly evaluate and select startup/project with greatest competitive advantage and/or most innovative (disruptive/exponential) business model
- o Understand and invest in pipe/platform startups with potentially highest Return On Investment and track their performance
- o Efficiently manage a portfolio of funded companies

❖ **Scalable Startups:** *Exponential (10X) Entrepreneur; Social Entrepreneur*
- o Rapidly prototype and evaluate alternative business models
- o Rapidly prepare, present, test, and manage the viability of a scalable business plan, startup, or project

- o Rapidly conduct experiments for viability of alternative business models especially using the Lean Startup Method
- o Solve customer pain and build innovative business model around the discovered solutions
- o Solve a Big Urgent Market Pain (BUMP)
- o Exploit technological innovation using innovative business models as well as value networks
- o Socially and economically transform a sector of society by using innovative/exponential business models in projects

❖ **Value Creators (Age 3+):** *Executive; Consultant; Designer; Intrapreneur; Entrepreneur*
- o Develop shared understanding of a business model
- o Create a "disruptive" or "blue ocean" strategy and business models in a legacy ("red ocean" or commoditized) industry
- o Translate a given strategy, job to get done, or value proposition into a coherent business model
- o Reconfigure existing business model or value chain
- o Sustainably increase profitability of enterprise or company
- o Facilitate achievement of sustainable competitive advantage especially by creating an ambidextrous organization
- o Facilitate mergers and acquisitions of companies
- o Improve quality or reduce defects of product/service
- o Improve or innovate on performance of existing process
- o Improve performance of non-profit organization
- o Improve sector of the economy such as in health care
- o Create culture of a "Customer-First organization (CFO)"
- o Prepare, review, improve, and/or manage career plan
- o Solve pain in any area of personal/business/national life

The key question now is: How well does the Business Model Canvas do when the respective customer segment "hires" it to get the above jobs done? In other words, what are the delight and pain experienced by the respective users while they get specific jobs done?

Although some perspectives about the trade-off and value of the Business Model Canvas are presented in Chapter ..., those views cannot be used to adequately answer the above questions. In theory, at least, interviews and ethnography studies should be conducted with the specific groups of users in order to obtain meaningful insights into the above questions. In the absence of such a "scientific" study, I provide my broad opinion which is based on my experience.

I first encountered the tool of the Business Model Canvas in March 2009. I even took part in the co-creation project for the Business Model Generation book in which the Business Model Canvas as fully featured. Since 2009, I've observed use of and widely experimented with the Business Model Canvas in many formats. Here are my impressions of the performance and value of the classic Business Model Canvas as it relates to the three types of customer segments.

Summary of Performance of Business Model Canvas

> **Financial Investors:** *Poor* Performance

> **Scalable Startups:** *Fair* Performance

> **Value Creators:** *Good* Performance

From above, the Business Model Canvas has the worst performance with Financial Investors. This observation is not very surprising since the Business Model Canvas and its associated tools were not originally designed for use by investors. Reasons for the poor performance of the Business Model Canvas include its non-obvious logic as well as lack of a broad lens for viewing the big picture of topics on the Business Model Canvas. In addition, absence of a linear format for the Business Model Canvas makes comparison and tracking of a portfolio of business models projects difficult.. Lastly, links or relationships between the financial aspects of a Business Model Canvas and those of a traditional business (financial) plan are not clear.

For today's scalable startups, the ultimate dream is to become a "unicorn" (startup with a billion dollar market capitalization within 10 years) or "exponential organization." The vast majority of unicorns or exponential organizations are platforms that have two or multi-sided markets. When it comes to presenting platforms on a Business Model Canvas, the diagram becomes unwieldy and difficult to read. The Business Model Canvas seems to be optimized for a single sided market.

With its 9 building blocks, the Business Model Canvas exclusively focuses on "Detailed Pain Discovery and Solving." For "Conceptual Pain Discovery and Solving" which involves rapid prototyping, fewer blocks may be required such as in using the format of a Meso-Canvas with 5 building blocks. Alternatively, a scalable linear diagram such as a Business Model

Strip – which uses four nodes and a "spine" - may be used. Unlike in the tool of the Business Model Canvas, the Business Model Strip can be easily applied for rapidly prototyping alternative platforms such as for unicorns, exponential enterprises, and non-profit organizations. Templates of two and multisided markets facilitate application of the Business Model Strips to platforms.

The Business Model Canvas has its best performance with Value Creators who are looking to document an existing business model either to gain clarity of how the business model works or to improve it. So far, the Business Model Canvas has not been directly applied for improving business processes. This task would seem outside the scope of tasks for a Business Model Canvas. However, the Business Model Canvas can easily be adapted for this purposed especially if it is used in conjunction with a Business Model Strip.

With the existing instructions and complementary tools for the Business Model Canvas, we can say that the Business Model Canvas is a good tool with instructions for use that can be greatly improve. The shortcomings of the Business Model Canvas are glaring when it is applied to platforms and in particular the health care sector. In order to widen areas of application of the Business Model Canvas as well as effectively and efficiently improve its usage, the following recommendations are made.

8 Tips for Improving Performance of the Business Model Canvas

1. Use a conceptual Business Model Canvas (Meso-canvas with 5 building locks) as well as detailed Business Model Canvas (Micro-canvas with 9 building blocks)
2. Use Business Model Strip with scalable number of topics
3. Use Business Model Design Process as presented within a Community Happiness Canvas that uses the Pain-Plan-Do-Review (PPDR) Cycle or POKER Cycle
4. Use the Lean Startup Method in conjunction with the conceptual/detailed Business Model Canvas as well as Business Model Strip
5. Use Exponential Business Canvas at conceptual/detailed level
6. Use ancillary tools such as Value Engine Map, Shared Value Map, SpaceTime Shared Value Map, COPS Diagram, …
7. Use Project Outcome Story Tree (POST) to monitor the progress of startup projects with inadequate data on project impact especially revenue
8. Use a Customer-First Business Model Canvas for customer-facing organizations

Although the Exponential Business Model Canvas is mentioned in the above tips, it has so far neither been explained nor presented. The Exponential Business Canvas involves translation of the logic and language of the Lean Startup Method into the 9-block layout of the Business Model Canvas. In order to understand the logic of the Exponential Business Strip which incorporates the Build-Measure-Learn (BML) Feedback Loop of the Lean Startup Method.

Exponential Business Strip (EBS)

PSQ: *How Might We Eliminate Pain (HMWEP) of X?*

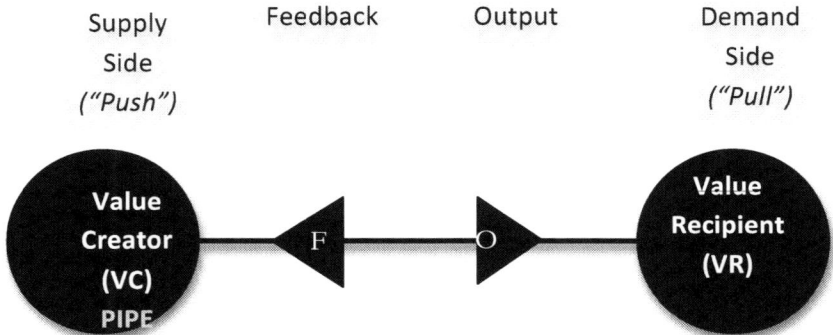

The four nodes of an Exponential Business Strip have the following elements, which are mainly described in the language of a Lean Startup:

- **Value Creator (VC):**
    - **Key Partners (KP):** Suppliers/Inputs
    - **Key Activities (KA):** Process (Activities/Tasks)
    - **Key Resources (KR):** People/Culture (Team/Resources: Unfair Advantages)
- **Feedback (F):**
    - **Cost Structure (C$):** Pain (Cost; Budget)
    - **Revenue Streams (R$):** Delight (Benefit; Revenue/ Pricing/Sale)
- **Output (O):**
    - **Value Proposition (VP):** Vision (Mission); Strategy (Goal/ Objective); Product/Service (Solution)
- **Value Recipient (VR):**
    - **Customer Segment (CS):** Customer Archetype
    - **Channels (CH):** Engines of Growth
    - **Customer Relationships (CR):** Key Metrics

In the graphics below, the Exponential Business Canvas is first presented at a meso-level with 5 blocks. Such a Conceptual Exponential Business Canvas is used when one is initially and quickly exploring a project idea or documenting a business model. This "big picture" view facilitates rapid exploration and testing of alternative business models without getting bogged down with details or "How?" or operational questions.

A Conceptual Exponential Business Canvas is useful for "extreme" rapid prototyping especially in the phase of Conceptual Design or Prefeasibility of Business Models. In other words, when searching for Problem-Solution Fit, it is advisable to use a Conceptual Exponential Business Canvas. Unlike in the Value Proposition Canvas, the Conceptual Exponential Business Canvas goes beyond Output ("Product") trade-off and Value Recipient ("Customer") trade-off; the Conceptual Exponential Business Canvas explicitly considers "Feedback" which may include validated business trade-off (strategy) and profit margin as well as "Revenue Streams." In this regard, the Conceptual Exponential Business Canvas is similar to Joan Magretta's "Value Proposition Triangle" which she discusses in her book, "Understanding Michael Porter." On a Conceptual Exponential Business Canvas, elements of a business model may, on demand, be zoomed into, zoomed out of, or added.

"Conceptual" Exponential Business Canvas (CEBC)
PSQ: *How Might We Eliminate Pain (HMWEP) of [High-end Music Lover]?*

5 Meso-Blocks

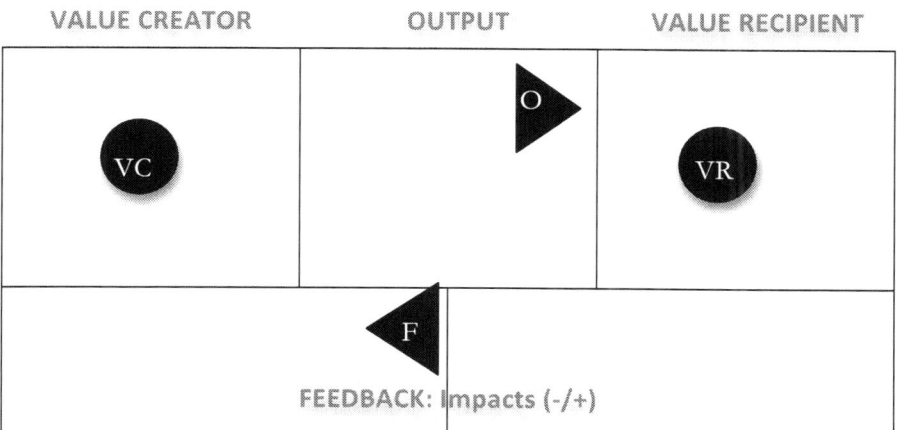

Once the logic of a business model is ascertained and documented at a conceptual level using the Conceptual Exponential Business Canvas, detailed documentation, testing, and validation can occur at the Feasibility Stage using a Detailed Exponential Business Canvas. The diagram below synthesizes, on one page, ideas and elements of the Lean Startup Method. It's important to note that as in the Conceptual Exponential Business Canvas, the primary focus of the Detailed Exponential Business Canvas is to iteratively answer the Pain Solving Question (PSQ).

"Detailed" Exponential Business Canvas (DEBC)

PSQ: *How Might We Eliminate Pain (HMWEP) of X?*

Key Partners (Suppliers/Input)	Process (Activities/Tasks)	Product/Service (10X-Solution: +/-; Analogs/Antilogs)	Engine of Growth (Channels/Marketing/Relationship	Customer Archetype (Job To Get Done; Delight: +; Pain: -)
	VC			VR
	People/Culture (Team/Resources: Unfair Advantages)	Strategy (10X-Goal/Objective/Value Proposition) Vision (10X-Mission)	Key Metrics ("Pirate" Metrics; KPI)	

PAIN (COST; BUDGET): - **DELIGHT** (BENEFIT; REVENUE (Pricing/Sale): +   F

Many processes exist for using a tool such as the Business Model Canvas or Exponential Business Canvas. Some processes have been discussed earlier; for instance, the Business Model Design Process using the framework of the Community Happiness Canvas. The core heuristic of every pain (problem) solving process, which involves a sense-and-respond feedback loop, is the PPDR Cycle: Pain-Plan-Do-Review (PPDR). Below are three steps for eliminating especially using a Business Model

3 Steps for Eliminating Pain: Using a Business Model Canvas or Exponential Business Canvas

Step 1 – USE PAIN SOLVING QUESTION (PSQ): Ask a Pain Solving Question (PSQ) in the format of "How Might We Eliminate Pain (HMWEP) of X?"
X refers to any object in a given system or ecosystem. Nevertheless, the most critical object or "weakest link", which is a bottleneck or constraint to a given goal of the system, must first be selected.

Step 2 - USE PPDR OR POKER CYCLE: Continuously answer, within a given time box,, frame, or "sprint", the PSQ by using in conjunction with the Pain-Plan-Do-Review (PPDR) or POKER Cycle the visual template of a business model pipe/platform; a Business Model Canvas or Exponential Business Canvas may be used.

Step 3 – DECIDE: Persevere, Pivot, or End: After a timebox or sprint ends, decide whether to persevere with eliminating the pain or pivot to another strategy or pain.
If "persevering," go to step 2. If "pivoting," go to step 1.
Otherwise, end pain solving exercise.

Finally, it is important to note that the Business Model Canvas implicitly follows the logic of a classic supply chain system with the supply side on the left hand side and demand (customer) on the right hand side. With customer-facing organizations, it may be easier to reverse the supply chain elements with the demand (customer) side on the left and supply side on the right. Although this change seems minor especially on a Business Model Strip, it could deeply impact how people think about and improve organizations. Indeed a change is mindset is involved from moving from an Enterprise-First Organization (EFO) to a Customer-First Organization (CFO). A Business Model Strip for a Customer First Organization is presented below.

Customer First Business Model Strip (CFBMS)
PSQ: *How Might We Eliminate Pain (HMWEP) of X?*

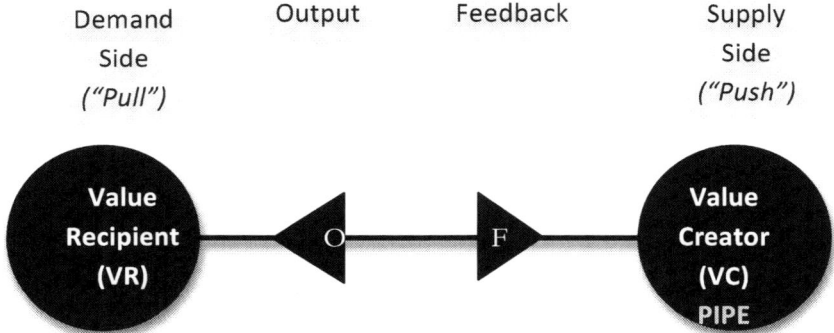

Here, a Customer First Business Model Canvas is presented.

Customer First Business Model Canvas (CFBMC)
PSQ: How Might We Eliminate Pain (HMWEP) of [High-end Music Lover]?

9 Micro-blocks

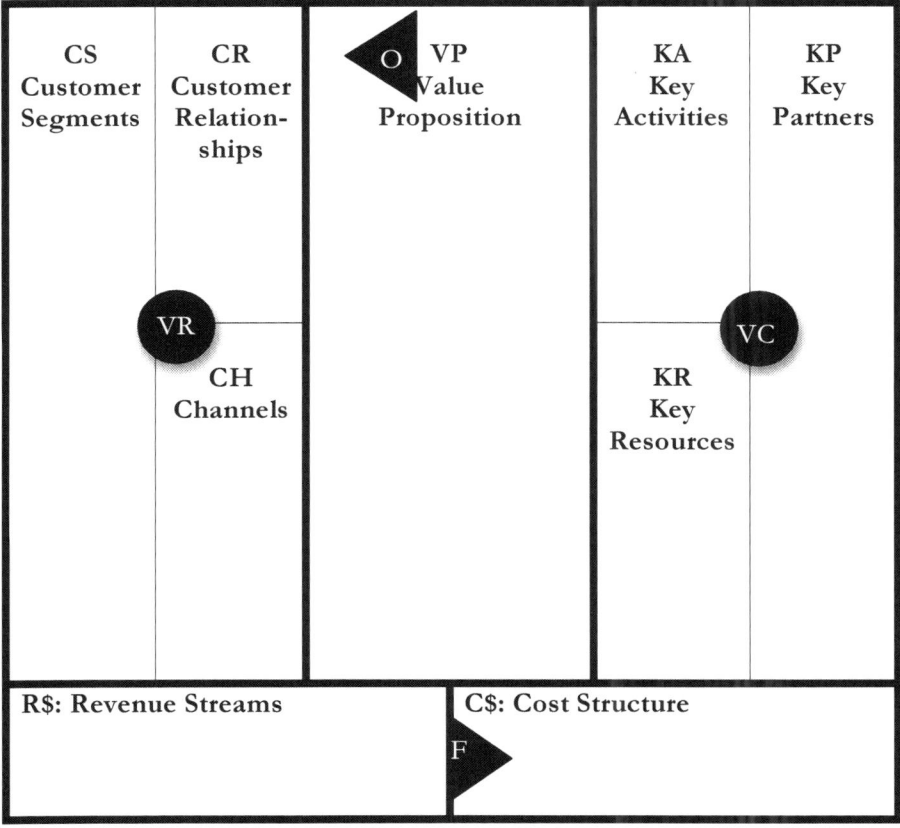

The following customer first canvas involves replacing topics of a Customer First Business Model Canvas with those from the Lean Startup Method. Also, some ideas are added from the perspective of Exponential or "10X" Organizations such as with regard to Vision and Strategy. A Customer First Exponential Canvas is presented below.

Customer First Exponential Business Canvas (CFEBC)

PSQ: *How Might We Eliminate Pain (HMWEP) of [High-end Music Lover]?*

9 Micro-Blocks

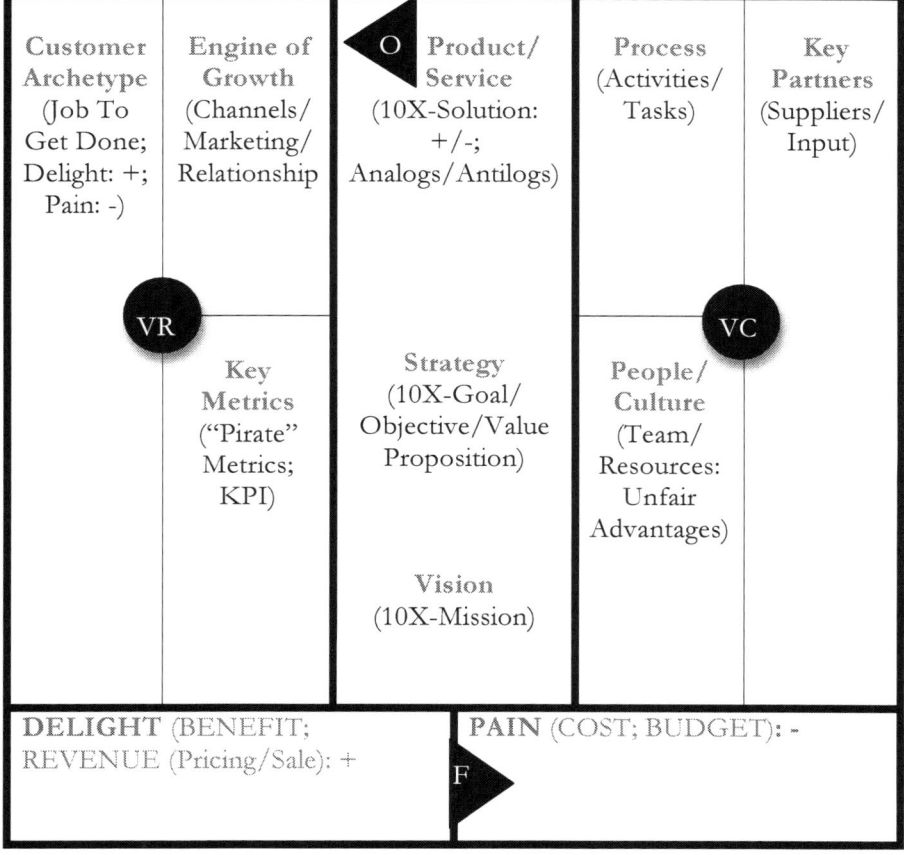

Customer Archetype (Job To Get Done; Delight: +; Pain: -)	Engine of Growth (Channels/ Marketing/ Relationship	O Product/ Service (10X-Solution: +/-; Analogs/Antilogs)	Process (Activities/ Tasks)	Key Partners (Suppliers/ Input)
	VR		VC	
	Key Metrics ("Pirate" Metrics; KPI)	Strategy (10X-Goal/ Objective/Value Proposition)	People/ Culture (Team/ Resources: Unfair Advantages)	
		Vision (10X-Mission)		

DELIGHT (BENEFIT; REVENUE (Pricing/Sale): +   **PAIN** (COST; BUDGET): -   F

EPILOGUE: BUSINESS MODEL POKER-SCORECARD FOR OPEN BUSINESS MODEL PROJECT MANAGEMENT (BMPM)

In today's environment of high volatility, uncertainty, complexity, and ambiguity, a disruptive era of project management is upon us without many people noticing. And like in the receding shoreline of an impending tsunami, many entrepreneurs, startups, and established organizations seem to be ignoring it. In business, the receding shoreline is the "closed" traditional and voluminous business plan that is rapidly being abandoned especially by startups. Established organizations are also questioning the wisdom of writing detailed long term plans for an environment that is rapidly changing. Even the US Military is transforming its planning paradigm to "Adaptive Planning & Execution (APEx)."

A *business model* is becoming the unit of project management in every domain. Consequently, displacing the traditional business plan as well as occupying its void are one page business modeling templates. The most popular business modeling templates are the Business Model Canvas and its derivatives such as the Mission Model Canvas and Personal Business Model Canvas notwithstanding the Lean Canvas by Ash Maurya. Due to the 9-block tessellated and non-linear graphic layout of these canvases, they share similar "handicaps" as the Business Model Canvas.

Absence of a visual linear template for the Business Model Canvas makes difficult the application of many business planning tools as well as tools of universal pain (problem) solving, design, and project management. Consequently, it is recommended that use of the Business Model Canvas be complemented with the Business Model Strip and tools of Open & Multilevel Pain Solving. In fact, it is advisable that a project starts with conceptual pain mapping, solution design, prototyping, and experimentation using a Business Model Strip. Thereafter, one can scale to detailed pain mapping, solution design, prototyping, and experimentation/ execution by using tools such as a Business Model Canvas.

As the business tsunami gathers momentum and approaches the shore, a field is emerging at the intersection of Open & Multilevel Pain Solving, Business Model Visualization, and Project Management. That field is called "Business Model Project Management (BMPM)." The goal of BMPM is to provide a shared visual language and integrated set of tools for instantly discovering and eliminating pains of stakeholders especially customers for an organization. The three "legs" of BMPM are the Business Model Strip (Canvas), Objectives & Key Results (OKR) Framework, and PPDR Cycle. The Framework for BMPM is illustrated below.

Business Model POKER Scorecard: Core Tool for Open Business Model Project Management (BMPM)

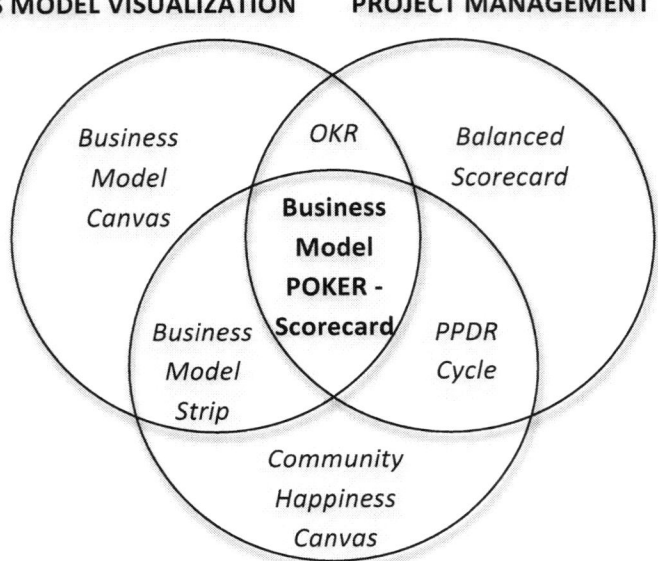

BUSINESS MODEL VISUALIZATION   PROJECT MANAGEMENT

Business Model Canvas

OKR

Balanced Scorecard

Business Model POKER - Scorecard

Business Model Strip

PPDR Cycle

Community Happiness Canvas

OPEN & MULTILEVEL PAIN SOLVING

In previous chapters, we focused on two "legs" of Business Model POKER Scorecard: Business Model Strip and PPDR (Pain-Plan-Do-Review) Cycle. However, we did not talk in depth about the third leg, which is the Objectives & Key Results (OKR) Framework.

The origin of the OKR framework can be traced to Peter Drucker's work in 1954 on the framework of "Management By Objectives (MBO)." However, MBO involves an elaborate top-down system of setting and achieving a hierarchy of goals throughout an organization. In 1974, Andy Grove of Intel created a simpler and more open (transparent) version of MBO and called the simplified framework "Objectives & Key Results (OKR)." Later, John Doerr, a former employee of Intel and who subsequently became a venture capitalist, introduced the OKR framework to Google in 1999. The present popularity of the OKR framework is due to use in and endorsement by highly successful Silicon Valley companies such as Intel, Oracle, Google, LinkedIn, Twitter, and Uber.

In brief, the OKR is a framework for rapidly defining and managing the performance of a *"line of business model,"* project, or experiment. Various heuristics exist for implementing the OKR framework in a project. A common heuristic can be described as the **3-3-3 OKR framework**: *formulate 3 objectives and 3 key results (outcomes) that should be achieved in 3 months for a given project, activity, or experiment.* The objectives should be "bold."

OKRs may be hierarchically prepared and integrated at multiple levels, for instance, at company, business unit (department), team, and employee levels. Organizations at lower levels in a hierarchy must contribute to the achievement of key results at a higher level as well as their own level. The diagram of the Business Model POKER Scorecard below, which is similar to a Strategy Map and Balanced Scorecard, presents a framework for facilitating Business Model Project Management with an emphasis on OKR. "POKER" is based on the Pain-Plan-Do-Review (PPDR) Cycle.

Business Model POKER-Scorecard *for 4 Categories of Business Model Pain*

Global Pain/Mission/Vision: .... Project Period: ....

BUSINESS MODEL *(Team)* **Scorecard**	VALUE CREATOR **(Value;** Finance)	FEEDBACK **(Learning;** Human Resources)	OUTPUT **(Product/ Service/VP;** Production)	VALUE RECIPIENT **(Customer;** Marketing)
Pain (Description)		◄F O		
Objectives *(Hypotheses)*				
Key Results *(Targets: Evidences/ Milestones/ Key Metrics)*				
Experi- ments (Projects/ To Do)				
Review *(Measures)*				

OKRs are usually made publicly available throughout an organization. Also, *intermediate results* can be reviewed frequently at intervals ranging from a weekly ("sprint") to monthly cycle. When using the Business Model POKER - Scorecard, it is important to distinguish between an "Enterprise–first" approach to OKRs and a "Customer-first" approach to OKRs. Enterprise-first approaches are internally, directly, and initially focused on the goal of business model profitability. They start with the goals, aspirations, and objectives of the Value Creator or Finance unit. In contrast, "Customer-first" approaches directly and initially focus on Value Recipients and the objective of creating awesome customer experiences. When properly implemented, an OKR Framework facilitates vertical alignment between a business unit or department's objectives (goals/strategy), resources, and actual results (success criteria) as well as horizontal (business model) alignment across business units or departments of an organization.

The Business Model POKER-Scorecard may be used to operationalize "Innovation Accounting" which is a system of business model performance (progress) management especially in the Lean Startup Method. It is important to point out, however, that the non-linear framework of the Business Model Canvas as well as its set of 9 business model topics makes it difficult to see the orthogonal relationship between topics of the Business Model Canvas and topics of OKR Framework or POKER. The apparently inseparable link between the 9 topics of the Business Model Canvas and its 9 building blocks/boxes acts like "blinkers" that restrict users from thinking out of the 9 boxes. This is in contrast to the Business Model Strip, where one can easily visualize a set of OKRs being developed for each topic of the Business Model Strip; see the Business Model POKER -Scorecard.

Since the structure of the Business Model Strip is central to the Business Model POKER-Scorecard, any business tool or methodology can be used in conjunction with the Business Model POKER-Scorecard. The Business Model OKR-Scorecard can even be used to do SWOT Analysis of a business model; see Appendix 4. Knowledge from use of the Business Model Canvas and its derivative tools can also be applied to the Business Model POKER-Scorecard. In particular, the Business Model POKER-Scorecard seamlessly meshes with topics that describe a business model as well as the Pain-Plan-Do-Review (PPDR) Cycle for pain solving. Hopefully, with a visual platform tool such as the Business Model POKER-Scorecard, we can rapidly build not only successful startups but also scale them into exponential organizations that eliminate some of the world's toughest pains.

Good luck!

BIBLIOGRAPHY

Blank, S.; Dorf, B. (2012) **The Startup Owner's Manual**. California: K & S Ranch, Inc.

Christensen, C.M.; Grossman, J.H.; Hwang, J. (2009) **The Innovator's Prescription**. New York: McGraw Hill.

Clark, T.; Osterwalder, A.; Pigneur, Y. (2012) **Business Model You**. New Jersey: John Wiley & Sons, Inc.

Deprez, F.L.; Tissen, R. (2002) **Zero Space**. San Francisco. Berrett-Koehler Publishers, Inc.

Gothelf, J.; Seiden, J. (2017) **Sense and Respond**. Boston: Harvard Business Review Press.

Maurya, A. (2012) **Running Lean**. California: O'Reilly Media.

Maurya, A. (2016) **Scaling Lean**. New York: Penguin.

Neely, A.; Adams, C.; Kennerley, M. (2002) **The Performance Prism**. London: Prentice Hall.

Osterwalder, A.(2004) **Business Model Ontology**. Lausanne: University of Lausanne.

Osterwalder, A.; Pigneur, Y. (2009) **Business Model Generation**. Amsterdam: Moddernman Drukwerk.

Osterwalder, A.; Pigneur, Y.; Bernarda, G.; Smith, A. (2014) **Value Proposition Design**. New Jersey: John Wiley & Sons, Inc.

Porter, M.E.; Teisberg, E.O. (2008) **Redefining Health Care**. Boston: Harvard Business School Press.

Ries, E. (2011) **The Lean Startup**. New York: Crown Business.

Smith, M.U. (Ed.) (1991) **Toward a Unified Theory of Problem Solving**. New Jersey: Lawrence Erlbaum Associates, Inc.

Weill, P.; Vitale, M.R. (2001) **Place to Place**. Boston: Harvard Business School Press.

Yeh, R.; Pearlson, K,; Kozmetsky, G. (2000) **Zero Time**. New York: John Wiley & Sons, Inc.

Wirtz, B. W. (2011) **Business Model Management**. Wiesbaden: Gabler.

APPENDICES

In the list of Appendices are additional tools for Business Model Project Management (BMPM) and Open & Multilevel Pain Solving (OMPS) as well as poems relating to the four nodes and perception o
f a Business Model Strip.

Appendix 1: Multilevel Canvas (Jigsaw, Tessellation, or TreeMap) System

Appendix 2: 4E-Multilevel Framework for Business Model Canvas

Appendix 3: True Logic of Business Model Canvas

Appendix 4: False Logic of Lean Canvas

Appendix 5: True Logic of Lean Canvas

Appendix 6: Mapping Topics of Templates for Business Model Innovation and Improvement (BMII)

Appendix 7: Templates for Business Model Project Management (BMPM)

Appendix 8: Anatomy of Ambidextrous Accounting

Appendix 9: Project Outcome Story Tree (POST)

Appendix 10: Fractal S-Wave for Multilevel Disruptive Innovation

Appendix 11: "Who's on First" Script

Appendix 12: "The Blind Men and the Elephant" Poem

APPENDIX 1: MULTILEVEL CANVAS (JIGSAW, TESSELLATION, OR TREEMAP) SYSTEM

Leve1 1: One-Block Canvas

Level 2: Three-Block Canvas *(Macro-Canvas)*

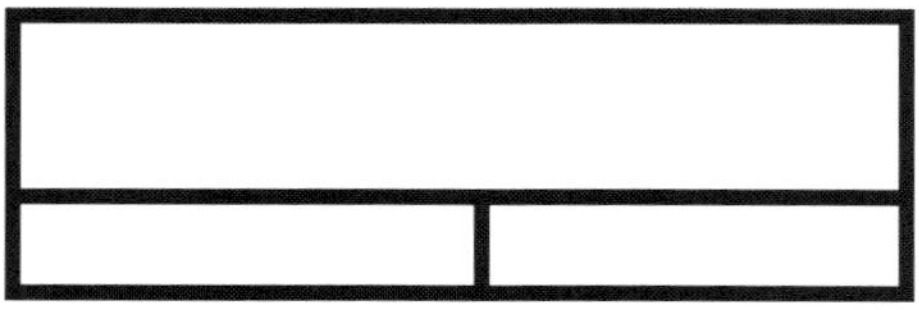

Level 3: Five-Block Canvas *(Meso-Canvas)*

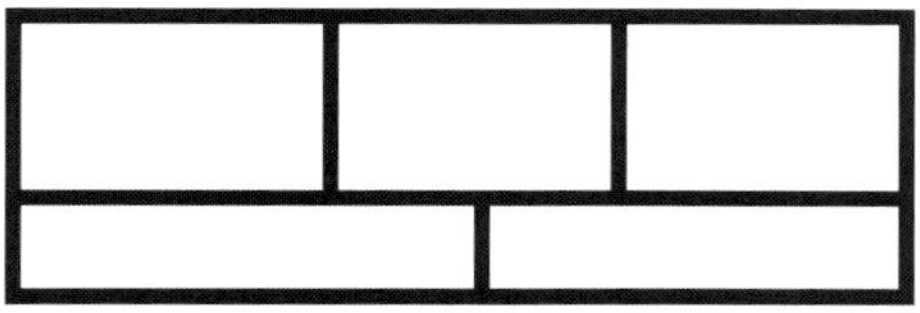

Level 4: Nine-Block Canvas *(Micro-Canvas)*

APPENDIX 2: 4E-MULTILEVEL FRAMEWORK FOR BUSINESS MODEL CANVAS

Shared Value Map: Multilevel Spatial Hierarchy of Enterprise, Ecosystem, Economy, and Environment (4E) *for Business Model Canvas*

WHEN: Future *(To Do)*/Present *(Doing)*/Past *(Done)*
Stakeholder: ....
Project Goal or Job To Get Done (JTGD): ....
Value: Benefit/Cost or **Delight/Pain (+/-)**.........................
Pain Solving Question (PSQ): ....
WHERE:

ENVIRONMENT
(Society/Government:
Local/Global)

Complementors

ECONOMY

Market
(Demanders)

ECOSYSTEM
(Sector; Segment)

EXTENDED ENTERPRISE
(SYSTEM: **Business Model**)

Competitors
(Startups or
Insurgents;
Substitutors or
Incumbents)

Industry
(Suppliers)

APPENDIX 3: TRUE LOGIC OF BUSINESS MODEL CANVAS

Business Model Canvas: True System Logic of Extended Enterprise or Supply Chain

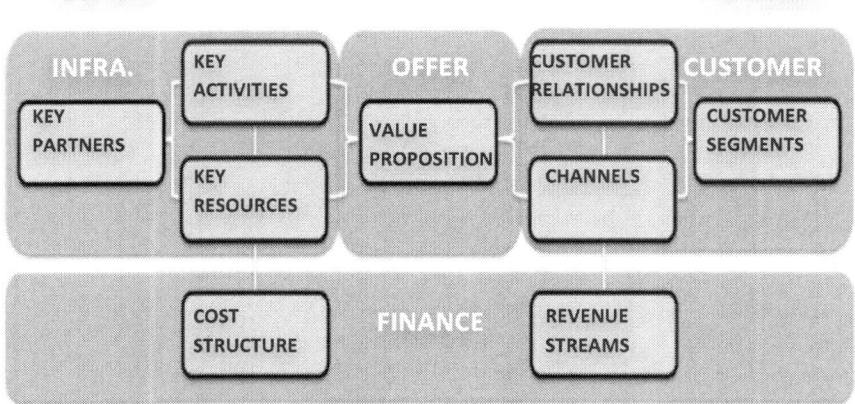

Business Model Canvas: True System Logic of Extended Enterprise or Supply Chain *(with 4 Superimposed Topics of Business Model Strip)*

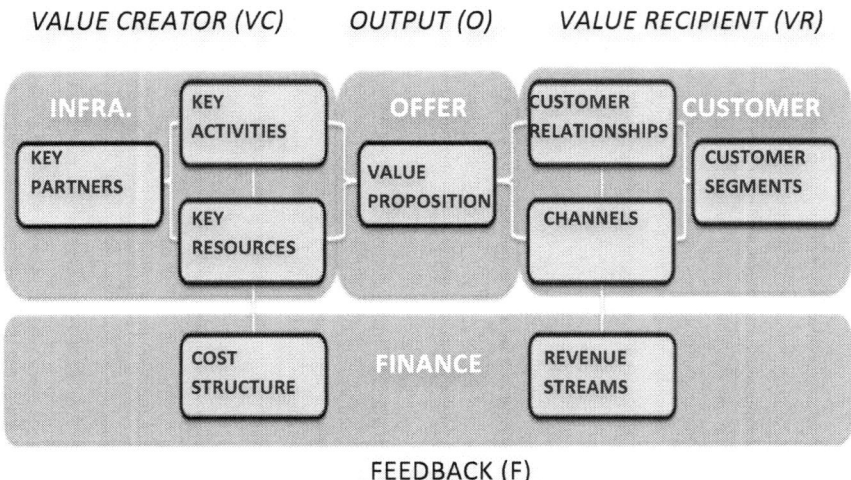

APPENDIX 4: FALSE LOGIC OF LEAN CANVAS

Lean Canvas: False System Logic of Extended Enterprise or Supply Chain

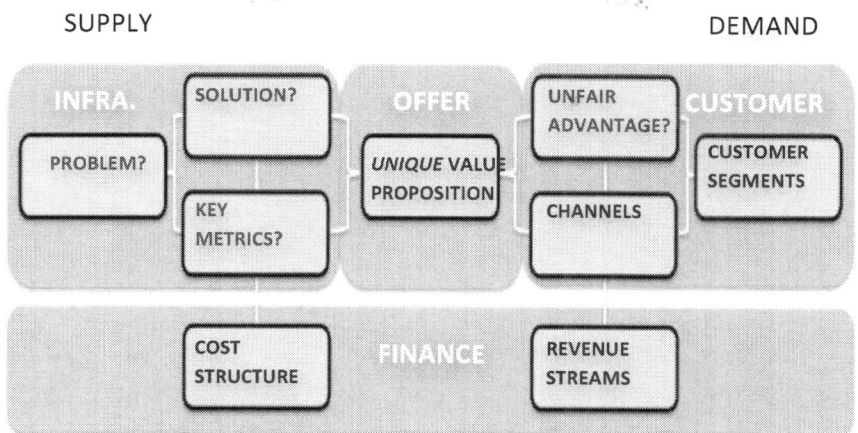

VALUE

(Impacts: -/+)

Lean Canvas: False Logic of Extended Enterprise or Supply Chain *(with 4 Superimposed Topics of Business Model Strip)*

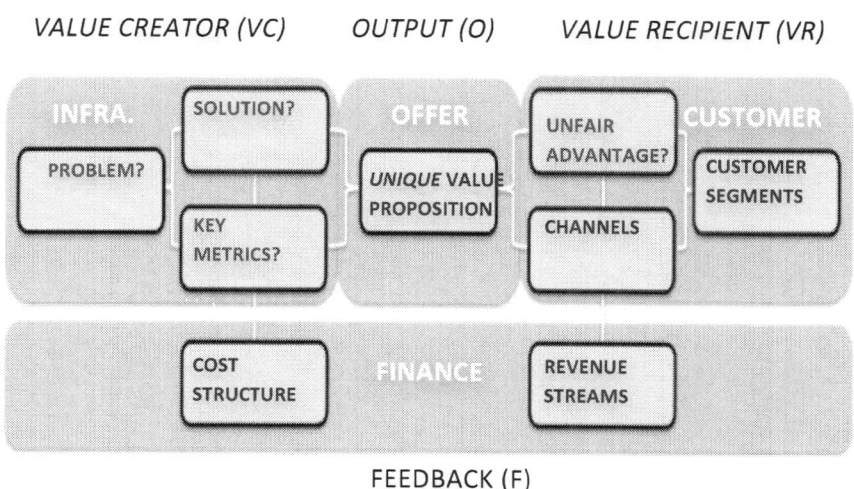

FEEDBACK (F)

(Impacts: -/+)

APPENDIX 5: TRUE LOGIC OF LEAN CANVAS

Lean Canvas: *True* System Logic of Extended Enterprise or Supply Chain

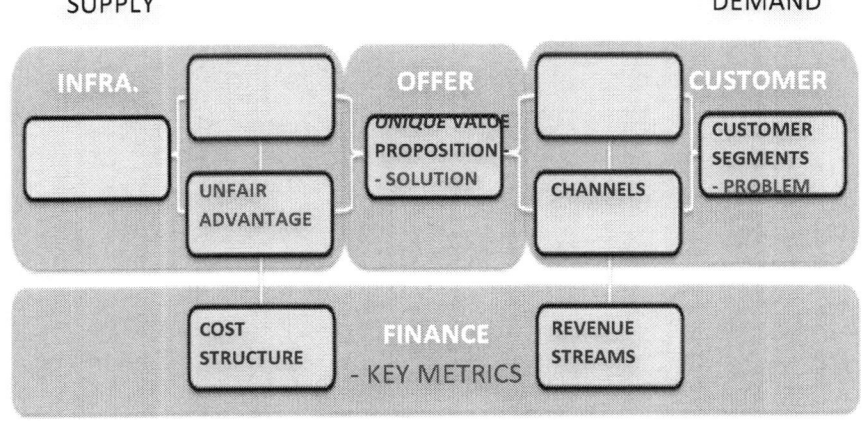

VALUE
(Impacts: -/+)

Lean Canvas: *True* System Logic of Extended Enterprise or Supply Chain *(with 4 Superimposed Topics of Business Model Strip)*

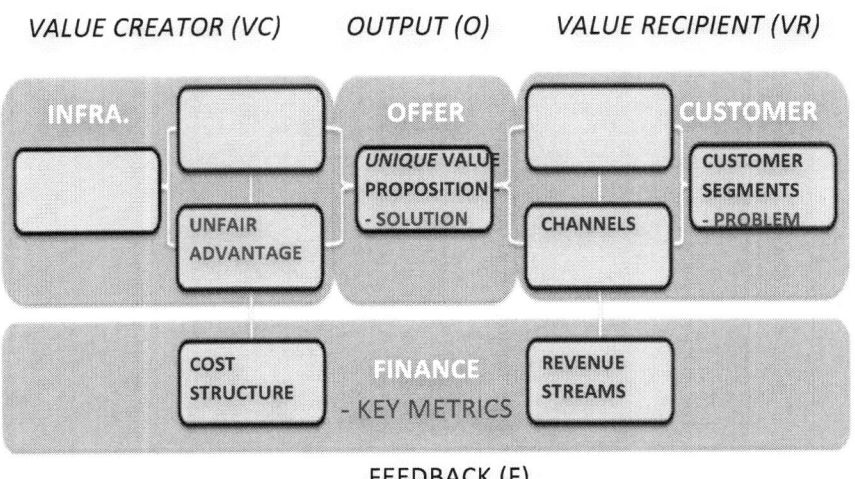

FEEDBACK (F)
(Impacts: -/+)

APPENDIX 6: MAPPING TOPICS OF TEMPLATES FOR BUSINESS MODEL INNOVATION AND IMPROVEMENT (BMII)

Business Model Strip for Organizing Tools & Topics in Business Model Innovation & Improvement: *Family of Business Modeling Tools*

How Might We Eliminate Pain (HMWEP) of X?

VALUE CREATOR (VC)	Feedback (F): Cue (-/+); UX; Revenue	Output (O): Offer (Product/ Service)	VALUE RECIPIENT (VR)
BUSINESS MODEL CANVAS: *9 Topics*			
Key Partners; Key Activities; Key Resources	Revenue Streams; Cost Structure	Value Proposition	Customer Segments; Customer Relationships; Channels
MISSION MODEL CANVAS: *9 Topics*			
Key Partners; Key Activities; Key Resources	*Budget (Cost)/ Mission Achievement (Fulfillment; Impact)*	Value Proposition	*Beneficiary/ Buy-in & Support/ Deployment*
VALUE PROPOSITION CANVAS: *8 Topics*			
		Product/ Service; *Functionality;* Gain Creators; Pain Relievers	*Customer Segment/Profile;* Job To Be Done; Gains; Pains
PERSONAL BUSINESS MODEL CANVAS: *9 Topics*			
Who Helps You; What You Do; Who You Are & What You Have	*What You Get; What You Give*	*How You Help*	*Who You Help; How You Interact; How They Know You & How You Deliver*

Business Model Strip for Organizing Tools & Topics in Business Model Innovation & Improvement: *Other Business Modeling Tools*

How Might We Eliminate Pain (HMWEP) of X?

VALUE CREATOR (VC)	Feedback (F): Cue (-/+); UX; Revenue	Output (O): Offer (Product/ Service)	VALUE RECIPIENT (VR)
4 PAIN SOLVING ACTORS: *4 Topics*			
HOW	WHY	WHAT	WHO
LEAN CANVAS: *9 Topics*			
Unfair Advantage	Revenue Streams; Cost Structure; *Key Metrics*	Unique Value Proposition	Customer Segments; *Problem; Solution;* Channels
4 BOX BUSINESS MODEL: *4 Topics*			
Key Processes; Key Resources	Profit Formula	Customer Value Proposition	
BUSINESS MODEL MAGIC TRIANGLE: *4 Topics*			
HOW (Value Chain)	WHY (Revenue Model)	WHAT (Value Proposition)	WHO (Customer Segment)
BCG BUSINESS MODEL DIAGRAM: *6 Topics*			
Value Chain; Organization	Revenue Model; Cost Model	Product/Service Offering	Target Segment
BALANCED SCORECARD: *4 Topics*			
Learning & Growth Persp.	Financial Perspective	Process Perspective	Customer Perspective

Business Model Strip for Organizing Tools & Topics in Business Model Innovation & Improvement: *Business Process Tools*

How Might We Eliminate Pain (HMWEP) of X?

VALUE CREATOR (VC)	Feedback (F): Cue (-/+); UX; Revenue	Output (O): Offer (Product/ Service)	VALUE RECIPIENT (VR)
PPDR CYCLE: *4 Topics*			
DO	REVIEW	PLAN	PAIN
KANBAN BOARD: *4 Topics*			
DOING	BACKLOG	TO DO	DONE
SIPOC DIAGRAM: *5 Topics*			
Supplier/ Input		Process; Output	Customer
DMAIC CYCLE: *5 Topics*			
Control		Improve	Define; Measure' Analyze
POKER SCORECARD: *5 Topics*			
Experiments	Review	Objectives Key Results	Pain
DESIGN SPRINT: *5 Topics*			
		Diverge; Decide; Prototype; Test	Understand
DESIGN THINKING: *6 Topics*			
Reflect		Ideate; Prototype; Test	Empathize; Define

APPENDIX 7: TEMPLATES FOR BUSINESS MODEL PROJECT MANAGEMENT (BMPM)

POKER-Scorecard *for Business Model Project Management*

Global Pain/Mission/Vision: ....….. Project Period: …….............…

POKER (Team) Scorecard	1	2	3	...
Pain				
Objectives (Hypotheses)				
Key Results (Targets/ To Do: Deliverables/ Evidences/ Key Metrics)				
Experi-ments/ Projects (Doing)				
Review (Progress)				

POKER-Scorecard *for Business Model Project Management*

Global Pain/Mission/Vision: .... Project Period: ....

POKER (Team) Scorecard	Quarter 1	Quarter 2	Quarter 3	Quarter 4
Pain				
Objectives *(Hypotheses)*				
Key Results *(Targets/ To Do: Milestones/ Evidences/ Key Metrics)*				
Experi-ments/ Projects *(Doing)*				
Review *(Progress)*				

POKER-Scorecard *for 4 Question-tags (Scene/Story)*

Global Pain/Mission/Vision: .... Project Period: ....

POKER *(Team)* **Scorecard**	**Question-tag**			
Pain	WHO			
Objectives *(Hypotheses)*	WHAT1			
Key Results *(Targets/ To Do: Milestones/ Evidences/ Key Metrics)*	WHAT2			
Experi- ments/ Projects *(Doing)*	HOW			
Review *(Progress)*	WHY			

POKER-Scorecard *for Business Tools Originating from Silicon Valley (USA)*

Global Pain/Mission/Vision: ....….. Project Period: ....…...……

TOOL POKER *(Team)* Scorecard	**Objectives & Key Results (OKR)**	**V2MOM**	**Lean Startup Method**	**Design Thinking**
Pain		Obstacles	(Customer Develop- ment)	*Empathize*
Objectives *(Hypotheses)*	Objectives	Vision	Vision/ Strategy	*Define*
Key Results *(Targets/* *To Do:* *Milestones/* *Evidences/* *Key Metrics)*	Key Results	Measures	Product	*Ideate*
Experi- ments/ Projects *(Doing)*		Methods Values	*Build/* *Measure*	*Prototype/* *Test*
Review *(Progress)*	(Grade: 0 – 1.0)		*Learn*	

Business Model Generic Scorecard *for 4 Categories of Business Model Pain*

Global Pain/Mission/Vision: .... Project Period: ....

BUSINESS MODEL *(Team)* **Scorecard**	VALUE CREATOR **(Value;** Finance)	FEEDBACK **(Learning;** Human Resources)	OUTPUT **(Product/ Service/VP;** Production)	VALUE RECIPIENT **(Customer;** Marketing)
Description		◀F ▶O		

Business Model POKER-Scorecard *for 4 Categories of Business Model Pain*

Global Pain/Mission/Vision: .... Project Period: ....

BUSINESS MODEL *(Team)* **Scorecard**	VALUE CREATOR **(Value;** Finance)	FEEDBACK **(Learning;** Human Resources)	OUTPUT **(Product/ Service/VP;** Production)	VALUE RECIPIENT **(Customer;** Marketing)
Description/ **Pain**		F O		
Objectives *(Hypotheses)*				
Key Results *(Targets/ To Do: Milestones/ Evidences/ Key Metrics)*				
Experi- ments/ Projects *(Doing)*				
Review *(Progress)*				

Business Model SWOT-Scorecard *for Business Model Project Management*

Global Pain/Mission/Vision: .... Project Period: ....

BUSINESS MODEL *(Team)* **Scorecard**	VALUE CREATOR **(Value;** Finance**)**	FEEDBACK **(Learning;** Human Resources**)**	OUTPUT **(Product/ Service/VP;** Production**)**	VALUE RECIPIENT **(Customer;** Marketing**)**
Description		◀F O▶		
S: Strengths				
W: Weaknesses				
O: Opportunities				
T: Threats				

Business Model Strategy-Scorecard *for Business Model Project Management*

Global Pain/Mission/Vision: .... Project Period: ....

BUSINESS MODEL *(Team)* **Scorecard**	VALUE CREATOR **(Value;** Finance)	FEEDBACK **(Learning;** Human Resources)	OUTPUT **(Product/ Service/VP;** Production)	VALUE RECIPIENT **(Customer;** Marketing)
Description/ Strategy		F ◀ ▶ O		
Means	Value	Progress	**End** **Ways**	User Experience

APPENDIX 8: ANATOMY OF AMBIDEXTROUS ACCOUNTING

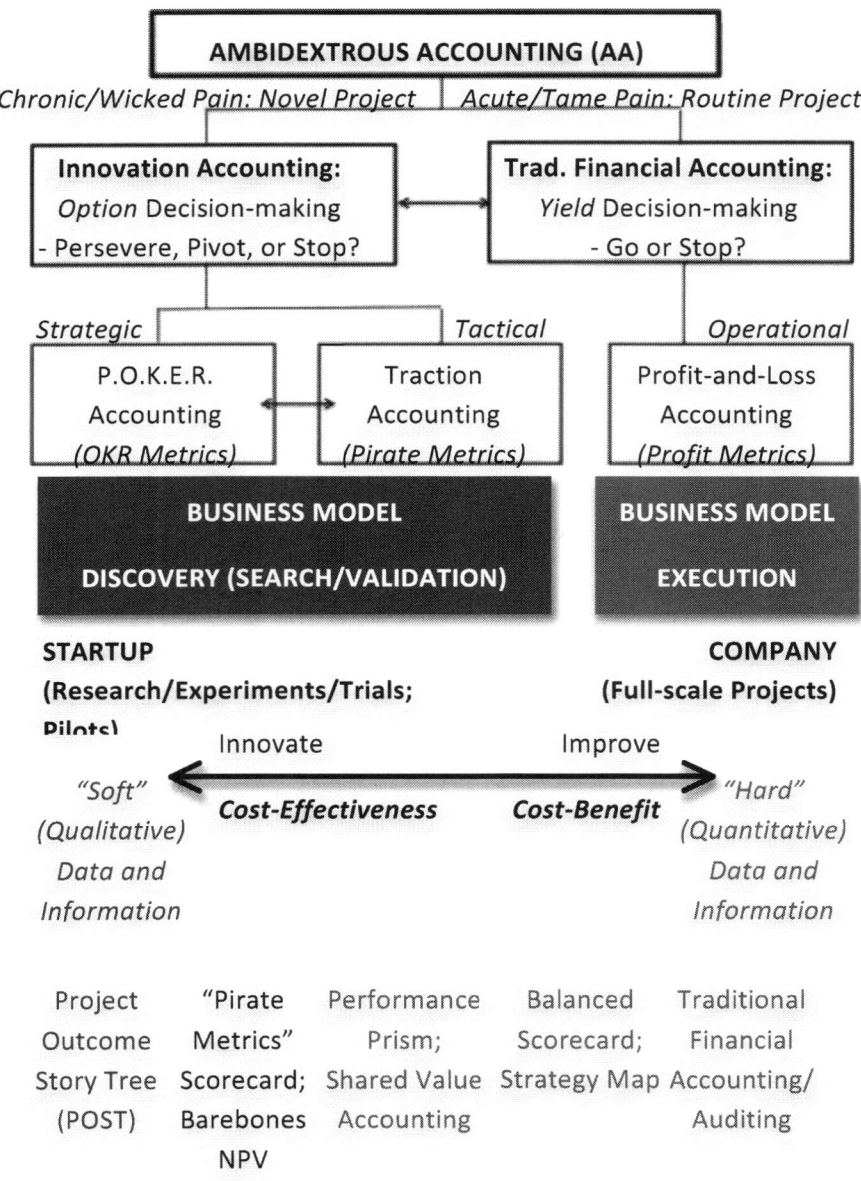

APPENDIX 9: PROJECT OUTCOME STORY TREE (POST)

Inspired by Kurt Vonnegut's "Shape of Stories," Option Financing Theory, and David Binetti's "Innovation Options" Framework, I developed the **Project Outcome Story Tree (POST)** as a *simple visual tool for tracking the progress of any (innovation) project for which data and information are sparse or unavailable.* The POST tool is applicable to many innovation projects where there is not enough data to quantify performance. The value or utility of Delight is assumed to vary from 0 to 1.0 while the value of utility of Pain varies from 0 to -1.0. Intermediate progress is measured using *"sprint" cycles.*

Using the POST Tool requires answering three questions:
◊ FUTURE: Where must the project performance go?
◊ PAST: Where was the project performance?
◊ PRESENT: Where currently is the project performance?
The POST tool can be used in conjunction with the Objectives & Key Results (OKR) Framework which requires grading at the end of a period such as in 3 months. Also, the POST tool is suitable for operationalizing the "Innovation Accounting" principle in the Lean Startup Method.

POKER-Scorecard *Illustrating the POST for POKER Innovation Accounting*
Pain: ....
Objective(s): ....
Key Result(s): ....
Experiment(s): ....
Review (Progress): ....

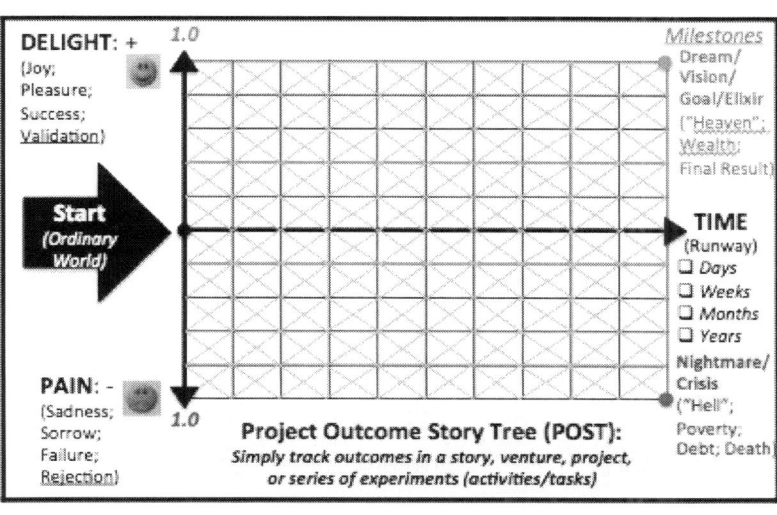

APPENDIX 10: FRACTAL S-WAVE FOR MULTILEVEL DISRUPTIVE INNOVATION

"Underdog vs. Top Dog" Disruption Theory

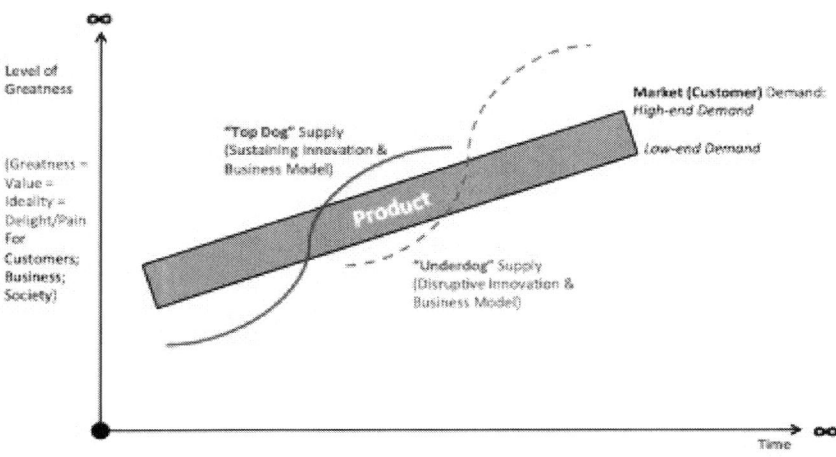

Fractal S-Wave

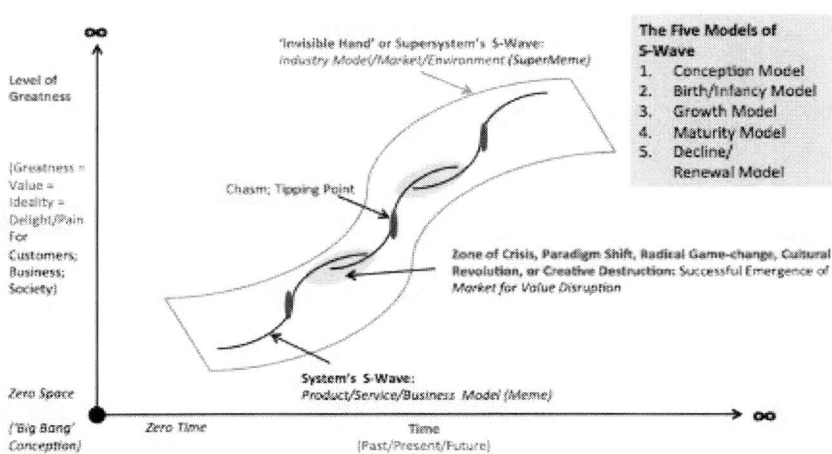

APPENDIX 11: "WHO'S ON FIRST" SCRIPT

Using Sports Analogies with the Business Model Strip (Diamond Format)

Business Model Strip in "Diamond" Format

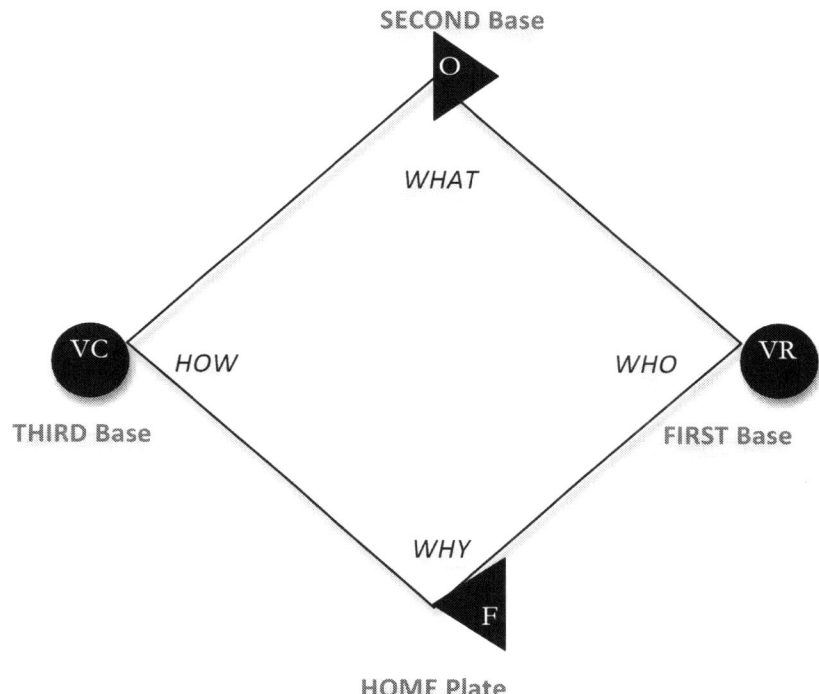

Script for "Who's on First"

(Lou Costello is considering becoming a ballplayer. Bud Abbott wants to make sure he knows what he's getting into.)

Abbott: Strange as it may seem, they give ball players nowadays very peculiar names.

Costello: Funny names?

Abbott: Nicknames, nicknames. Now, on the St. Louis team we have Who's on first, What's on second, I Don't Know is on third--

Costello: That's what I want to find out. I want you to tell me the names of the fellows on the St. Louis team.

Abbott: I'm telling you. Who's on first, What's on second, I Don't Know is on third--

Costello: You know the fellows' names?

Abbott: Yes.

Costello: Well, then who's playing first?

Abbott: Yes.

Costello: I mean the fellow's name on first base.

Abbott: Who.

Costello: The fellow playin' first base.

Abbott: Who.

Costello: The guy on first base.

Abbott: Who is on first.

Costello: Well, what are you askin' me for?

Abbott: I'm not asking you--I'm telling you. Who is on first.

Costello: I'm asking you--who's on first?

Abbott: That's the man's name.

Costello: That's who's name?

Abbott: Yes.

~ ~ ~ ~ ~

Costello: St. Louis has a good outfield?

Abbott: Oh, absolutely.

Costello: The left fielder's name?

Abbott: Why.

Costello: I don't know, I just thought I'd ask.

Abbott: Well, I just thought I'd tell you.

Costello: Then tell me who's playing left field?

Abbott: Who's playing first.

Costello: Stay out of the infield! The left fielder's name?

Abbott: Why.

Costello: Because.

Abbott: Oh, he's center field.

Costello: Wait a minute. You got a pitcher on this team?

Abbott: Wouldn't this be a fine team w i t h o u t a pitcher?

Costello: Tell me the pitcher's name.

Abbott: Tomorrow.

~ ~ ~ ~ ~

Costello: Now, when the guy at bat bunts the ball--me being a good catcher--I want to throw the guy out at first base, so I pick up the ball and throw it to who?

Abbott: Now, that's he first thing you've said right.

Costello: I DON'T EVEN KNOW WHAT I'M TALKING ABOUT!

Abbott: Don't get excited. Take it easy.

Costello: I throw the ball to first base, whoever it is grabs the ball, so the guy runs to second. Who picks up the ball and throws it to what. What throws it to I don't know. I don't know throws it back to tomorrow--a triple play.

Abbott: Yeah, it could be.

Costello: Another guy gets up and it's a long ball to center.

Abbott: Because.

Costello: Why? I don't know. And I don't care.

Abbott: What was that?

Costello: I said, I DON'T CARE!

Abbott: Oh, that's our shortstop!

Source: http://www.psu.edu/dept/inart10_110/inart10/whos.html

APPENDIX 12: "THE BLIND MEN AND THE ELEPHANT" Poem

The Blind Men and the Elephant
John Godfrey Saxe (1816-1887)

It was six men of Indostan
To learning much inclined,
Who went to see the Elephant
(Though all of them were blind),
That each by observation
Might satisfy his mind.

The *First* approached the Elephant,
And happening to fall
Against his broad and sturdy side,
At once began to bawl:
"God bless me! but the Elephant
Is very like a WALL!"

The *Second*, feeling of the tusk,
Cried, "Ho, what have we here,
So very round and smooth and sharp?
To me 'tis mighty clear
This wonder of an Elephant
Is very like a SPEAR!"

The *Third* approached the animal,
And happening to take
The squirming trunk within his hands,
Thus boldly up and spake:
"I see," quoth he, "the Elephant
Is very like a SNAKE!"

The *Fourth* reached out an eager hand,
And felt about the knee
"What most this wondrous beast is like
Is mighty plain," quoth he:
"'Tis clear enough the Elephant
Is very like a TREE!"

Fifth, who chanced to touch the ear,
Said: "E'en the blindest man
Can tell what this resembles most;
Deny the fact who can,
This marvel of an Elephant
Is very like a FAN!"

The *Sixth* no sooner had begun
About the beast to grope,
Than seizing on the swinging tail
That fell within his scope,
"I see," quoth he, "the Elephant
Is very like a ROPE!"

And so these men of Indostan
Disputed loud and long,
Each in his own opinion
Exceeding stiff and strong,
Though each was partly in the right,
And all were in the wrong!

ABOUT THE AUTHOR, ROD KING

Rod King, PhD, (aka "SiliconValleyRebel") is a world-class expert on creativity, innovation, and strategy as well as a prolific inventor of tools for business modeling and performance management. He is the inventor of the business platform tool of the **POKER-Scorecard**, which provides a shared language for collaboratively answering every Pain Solving Question. The POKER-Scorecard is a one-page visual template that can be used for rapidly presenting and applying diverse tools including the Business Model Canvas, Lean Canvas, and Balanced Scorecard as well as the OKR Framework, V2MOM Framework, Design Thinking, and Lean Startup Method. In simple terms, the POKER-Scorecard is a "one-in-all" platform tool that disrupts the paradigm of *"one tool does not fit all."* The POKER Canvas is a "jigsaw" template of the POKER Scorecard.

Dr. King provides consulting, coaching, and training services as well as seminars to **"exponential (10X) thinking" entrepreneurs, teams, startups, and organizations**. In particular, he facilitates the methodology of *Ambidextrous Accounting* which combines collaborative business modeling with tools of the Pain-Plan-Do-Review (PPDR) or POKER Learning Cycle and Performance Management. He also focuses on applying business modeling (platform) techniques to areas such as *healthcare and non-profit organizations* where existing "pipe-focused" business modeling tools such as the Business Model Canvas and Lean Canvas are grossly inadequate.

Dr. King is also an advocate for and a practitioner of the paradigm of Genius Innovation & Polymathism (GIP). Dr. King is on a mission to make tools of GIP such as the POKER-Scorecard available to everyone on the planet. Everyone should unleash their potential while becoming a "Genius Innovator & Polymath (GIP)." By the way, POKER is an acronym for Pain-Objectives-Key Results-Experiments-Review. The POKER cycle is an expression of the sense-and-respond feedback loop which is at the heart of every rapid pain solving and learning system. Dr. King believes that with mastery of the POKER-Scorecard and its application using the collaboration paradigm of Open & Multilevel Pain Solving, we can more rapidly eliminate every "acute" and "chronic" pain while building **exponential organizations**.

Hobbies of Dr. King include playing ping pong and chess as well as inventing and performing conjuring tricks. Also, he holds a US and International Patent Pending for his invention of the Fractal Grid Technology or "Infinitely Zoomable 3x3 Interface."

Dr. Rod King can be reached at rodkuhnhking@gmail.com.

Also, feel free to connect with Dr. King
on Twitter (@rodkuhnking and #SiliconValleyRebel)) as well as

on LinkedIn (https://www.linkedin.com/in/rodkuhnking/)

Your feedback is greatly appreciated especially regarding this book and
your application of its tools.

DISRUPT TRADITIONAL ENTREPRENEURIAL TRAINING
IN
SILICON VALLEY & THE REST OF THE WORLD

Join the Movement for **Exponential Thinking Entrepreneurs (ETE)**

#SiliconValleyRebel

Printed in Great Britain
by Amazon